DOCTOR RADAR

TITAN
COMICS

DOCTOR RADAR

WRITTEN BY
NOËL SIMSOLO

ART BY
BÉZIAN

TRANSLATED BY
IVANKA HAHNENBERGER

Titan
COMICS

DOCTOR RADAR
ISBN:9781785863936

Published by Titan Comics
A division of Titan Publishing Group Ltd.
144 Southwark St.
London
SE1 0UP

Originally published in French as: Docteur Radar © Éditions Glénat 2014.
All rights reserved.

A CIP catalogue record for this title is available from the
British Library.

First edition: April 2018

10 9 8 7 6 5 4 3 2 1

Printed in China.

www.titan-comics.com
Follow us on Twitter @ComicsTitan
Visit us at facebook.com/comicstitan

TITAN COMICS

COLLECTION EDITOR
JONATHAN STEVENSON

MANAGING & LAUNCH EDITOR
ANDREW JAMES

DESIGNER
WILFRIED
TSHIKANA-EKUTSHU

PRODUCTION ASSISTANT
NATALIE BOLGER

PRODUCTION SUPERVISOR
MARIA PEARSON

PRODUCTION CONTROLLER
PETER JAMES

SENIOR PRODUCTION CONTROLLER
JACKIE FLOOK

ART DIRECTOR
OZ BROWNE

SENIOR SALES MANAGER
STEVE TOTHILL

CIRCULATION ASSISTANT
FRANCES HALLAM

PRESS OFFICER
WILL O'MULLANE

BRAND MANAGER
CHRIS THOMPSON

ADS & MARKETING ASSISSTANT
TOM MILLER

DIRECT SALES &
MARKETING MANAGER
RICKY CLAYDON

COMMERCIAL MANAGER
MICHELLE FAIRLAMB

PUBLISHING MANAGER
DARRYL TOTHILL

PUBLISHING DIRECTOR
CHRIS TEATHER

OPERATIONS DIRECTOR
LEIGH BAULCH

EXECUTIVE DIRECTOR
VIVIAN CHEUNG

PUBLISHER
NICK LANDAU

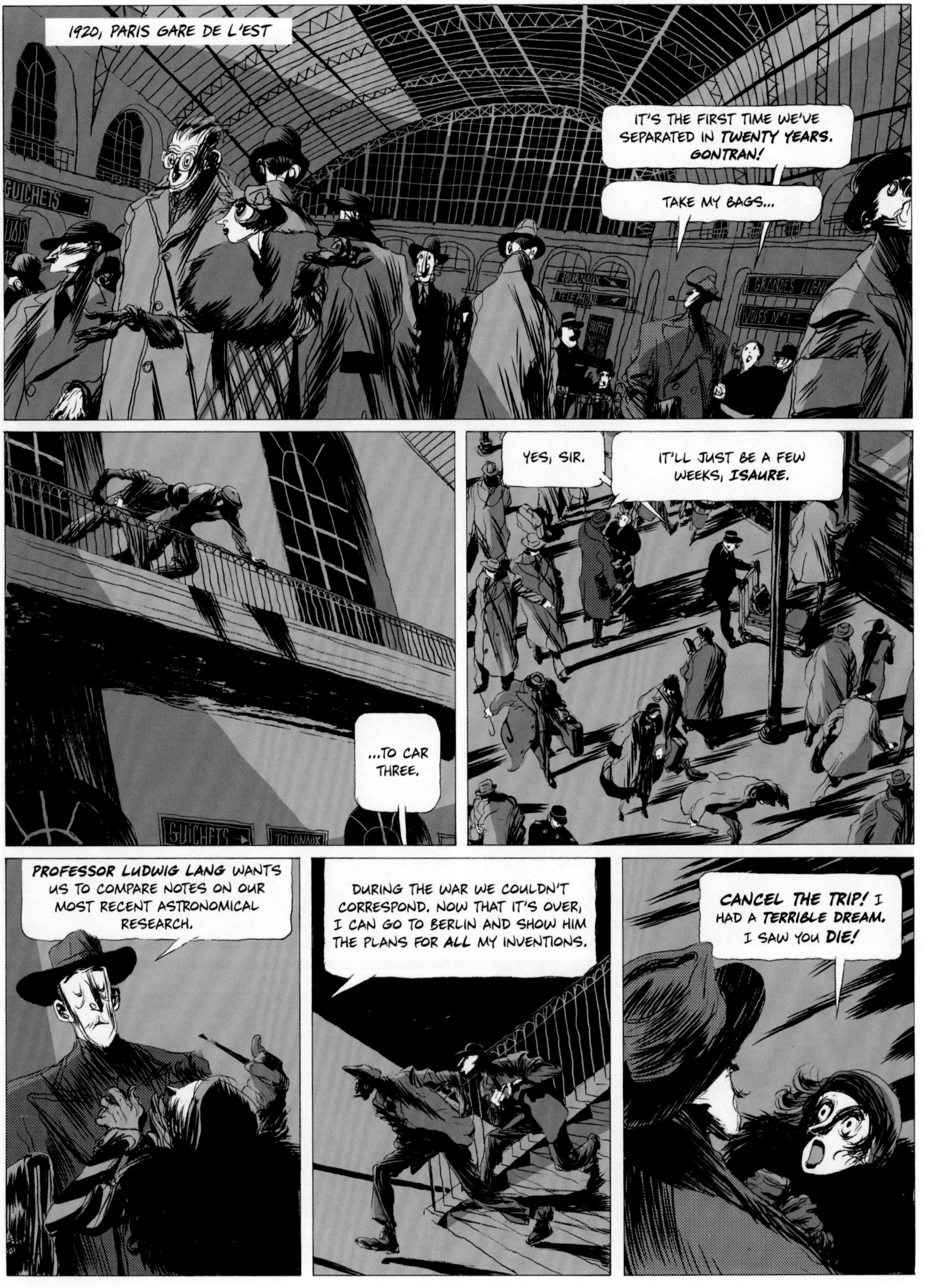

1920, PARIS GARE DE L'EST
GUICHETS
JOURNAUX
TELEPHONE
BUFFET
IT'S THE FIRST TIME WE'VE SEPARATED IN **TWENTY YEARS**, **GONTRAN!**
TAKE MY BAGS...
...TO CAR THREE.
GUICHETS
YES, SIR.
IT'LL JUST BE A FEW WEEKS, **ISAURE.**
PROFESSOR LUDWIG LANG WANTS US TO COMPARE NOTES ON OUR MOST RECENT ASTRONOMICAL RESEARCH.
DURING THE WAR WE COULDN'T CORRESPOND. NOW THAT IT'S OVER, I CAN GO TO BERLIN AND SHOW HIM THE PLANS FOR **ALL** MY INVENTIONS.
CANCEL THE TRIP! I HAD A **TERRIBLE DREAM.** I SAW YOU **DIE!**

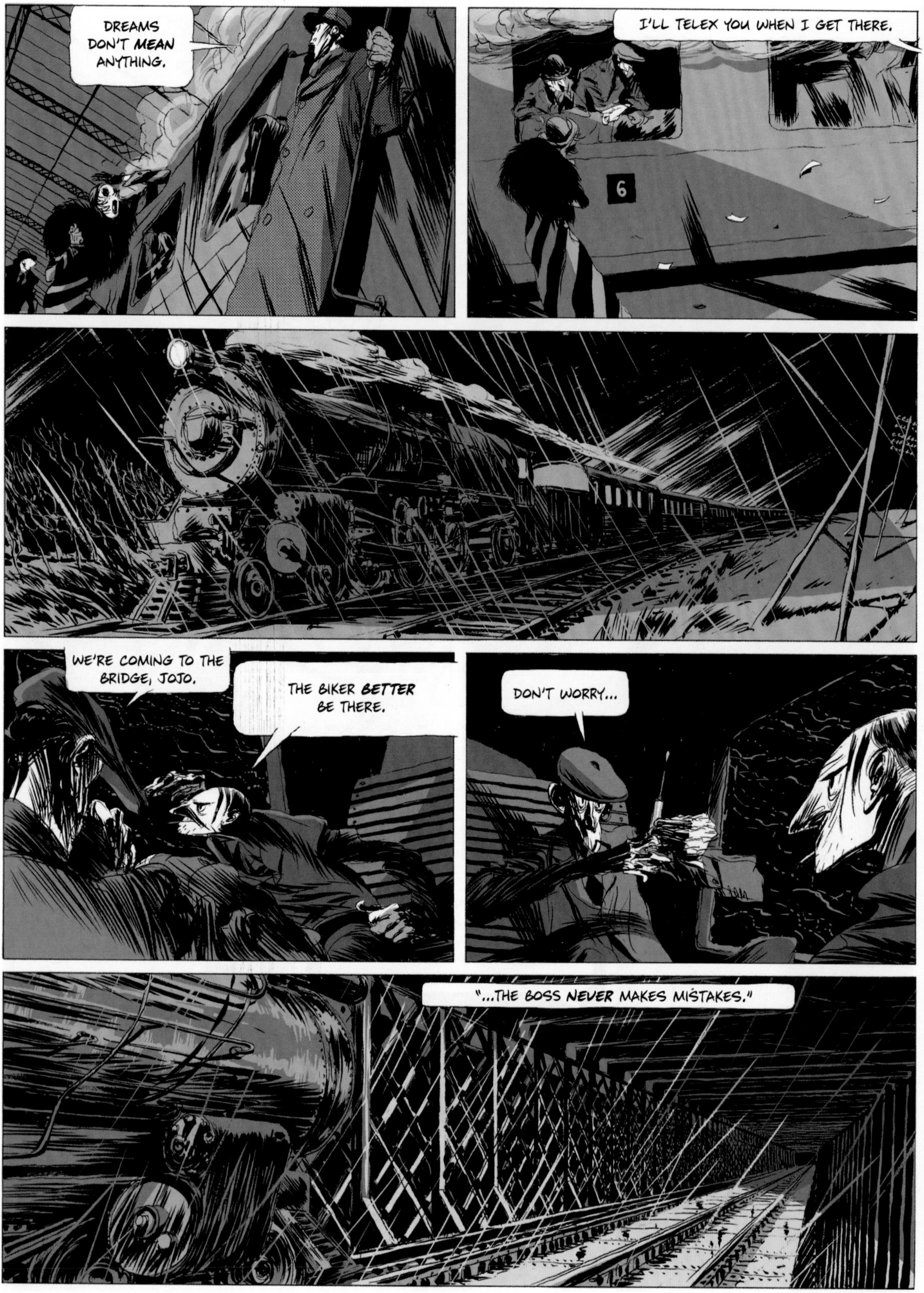
DREAMS DON'T MEAN ANYTHING.
I'LL TELEX YOU WHEN I GET THERE.
6
WE'RE COMING TO THE BRIDGE, JOJO.
THE BIKER BETTER BE THERE.
DON'T WORRY...
"...THE BOSS NEVER MAKES MISTAKES."

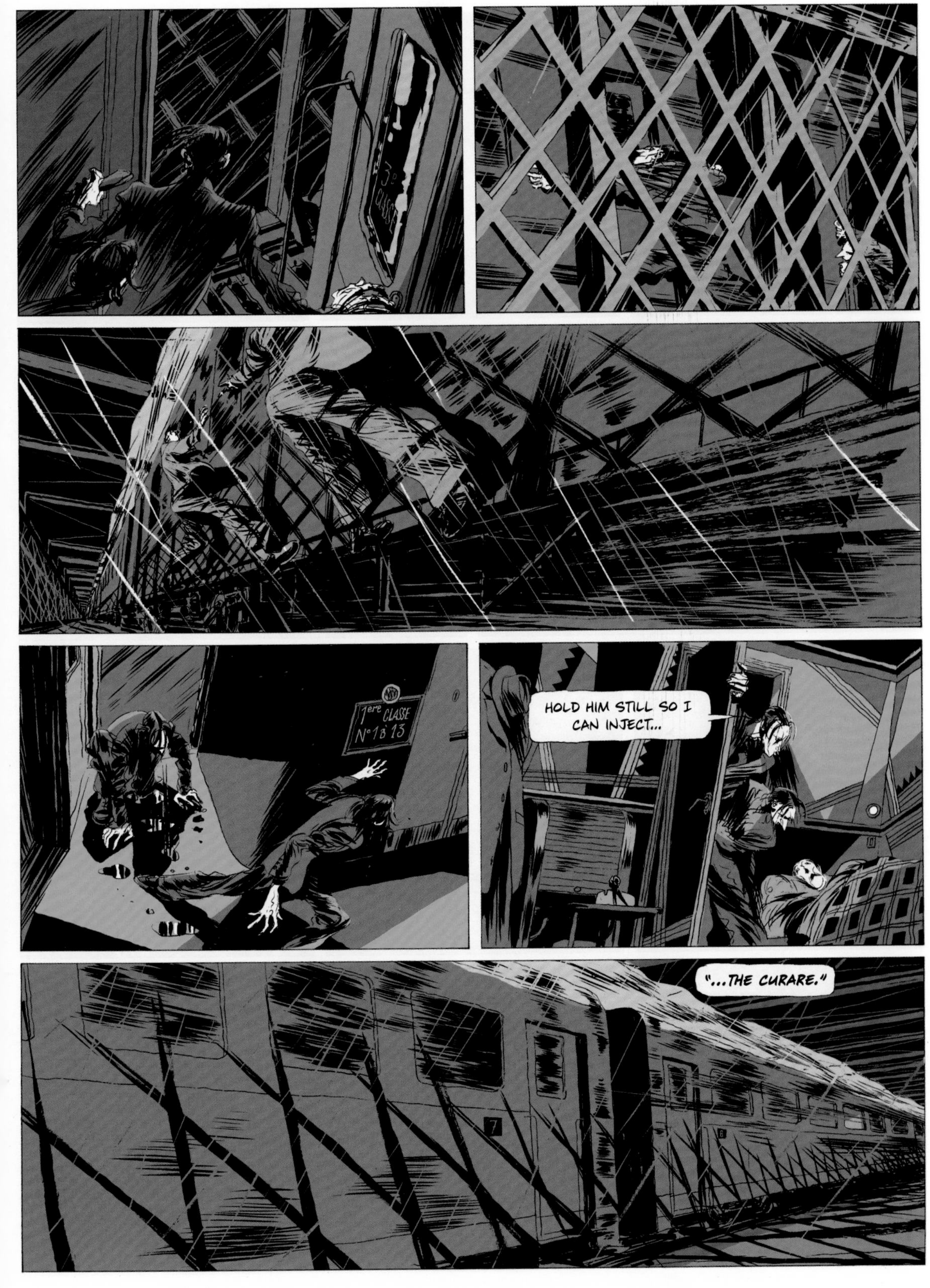
HOLD HIM STILL SO I CAN INJECT...
"...THE CURARE."

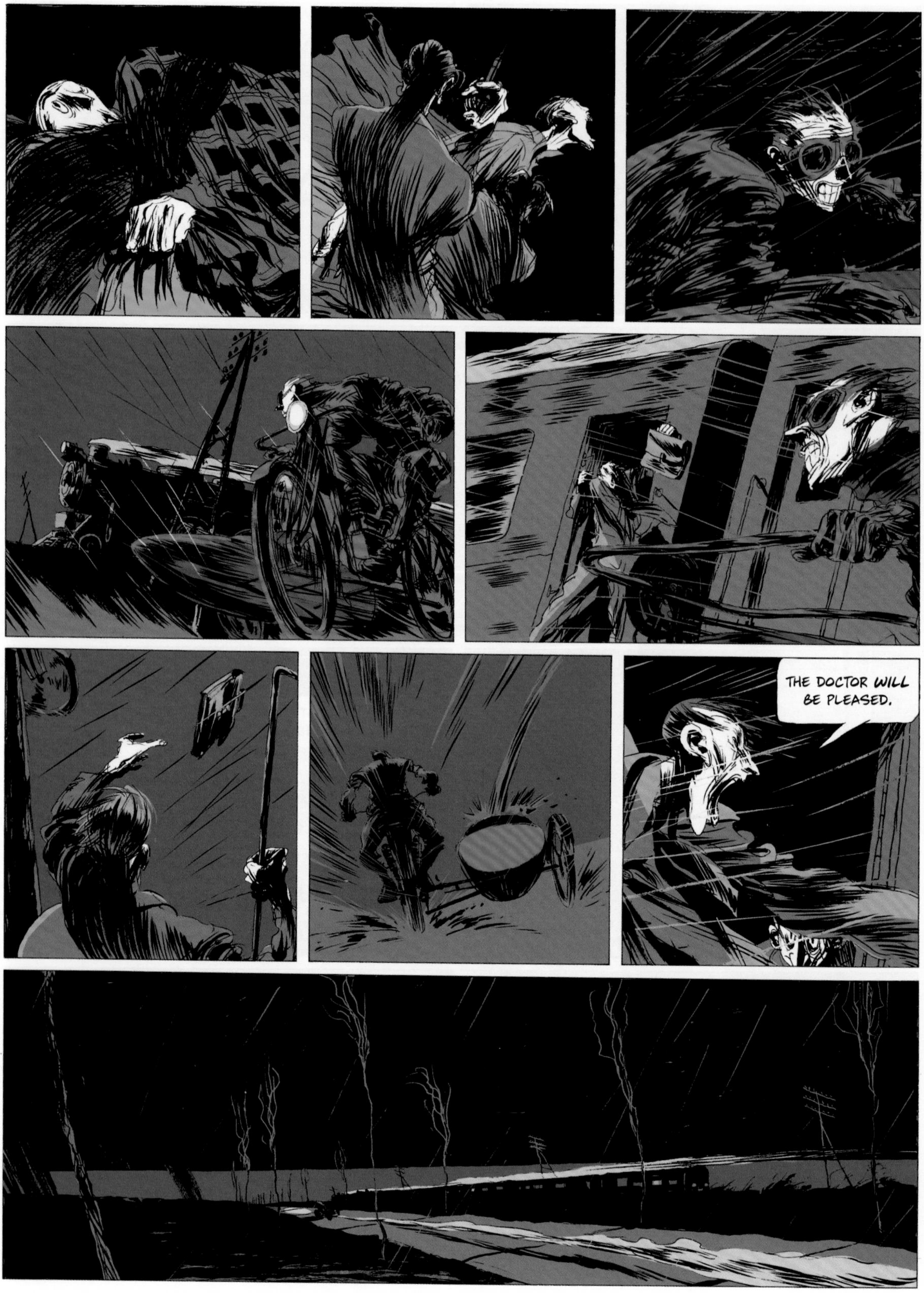
THE DOCTOR WILL
BE PLEASED.

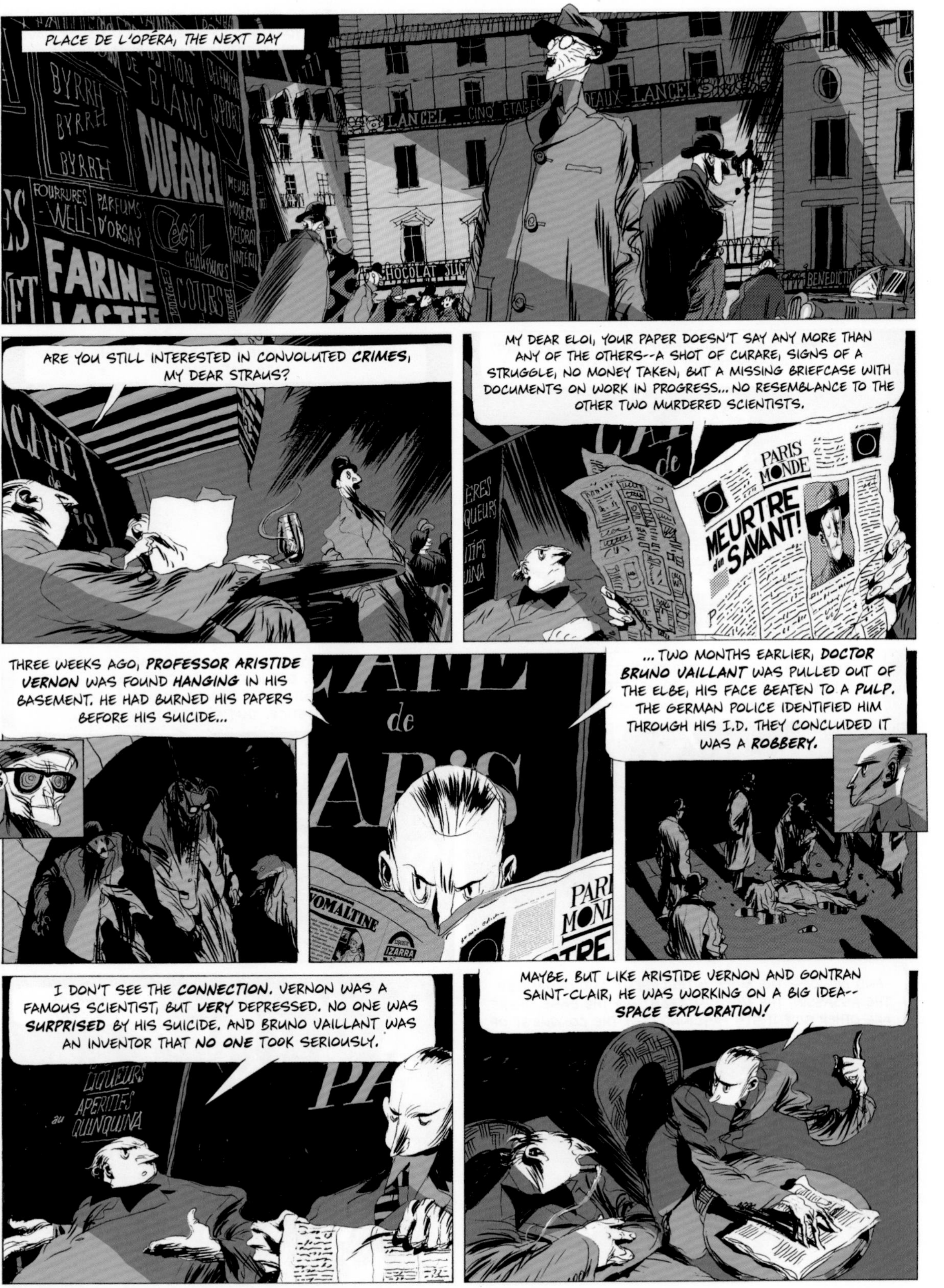
PLACE DE L'OPÉRA, THE NEXT DAY
ARE YOU STILL INTERESTED IN CONVOLUTED CRIMES, MY DEAR STRAUS?
MY DEAR ELOI, YOUR PAPER DOESN'T SAY ANY MORE THAN ANY OF THE OTHERS--A SHOT OF CURARE, SIGNS OF A STRUGGLE, NO MONEY TAKEN, BUT A MISSING BRIEFCASE WITH DOCUMENTS ON WORK IN PROGRESS... NO RESEMBLANCE TO THE OTHER TWO MURDERED SCIENTISTS.
PARIS MONDE
MEURTRE d'un SAVANT!
THREE WEEKS AGO, PROFESSOR ARISTIDE VERNON WAS FOUND HANGING IN HIS BASEMENT. HE HAD BURNED HIS PAPERS BEFORE HIS SUICIDE...
...TWO MONTHS EARLIER, DOCTOR BRUNO VAILLANT WAS PULLED OUT OF THE ELBE, HIS FACE BEATEN TO A PULP. THE GERMAN POLICE IDENTIFIED HIM THROUGH HIS I.D. THEY CONCLUDED IT WAS A ROBBERY.
I DON'T SEE THE CONNECTION. VERNON WAS A FAMOUS SCIENTIST, BUT VERY DEPRESSED. NO ONE WAS SURPRISED BY HIS SUICIDE. AND BRUNO VAILLANT WAS AN INVENTOR THAT NO ONE TOOK SERIOUSLY.
MAYBE. BUT LIKE ARISTIDE VERNON AND GONTRAN SAINT-CLAIR, HE WAS WORKING ON A BIG IDEA--SPACE EXPLORATION!

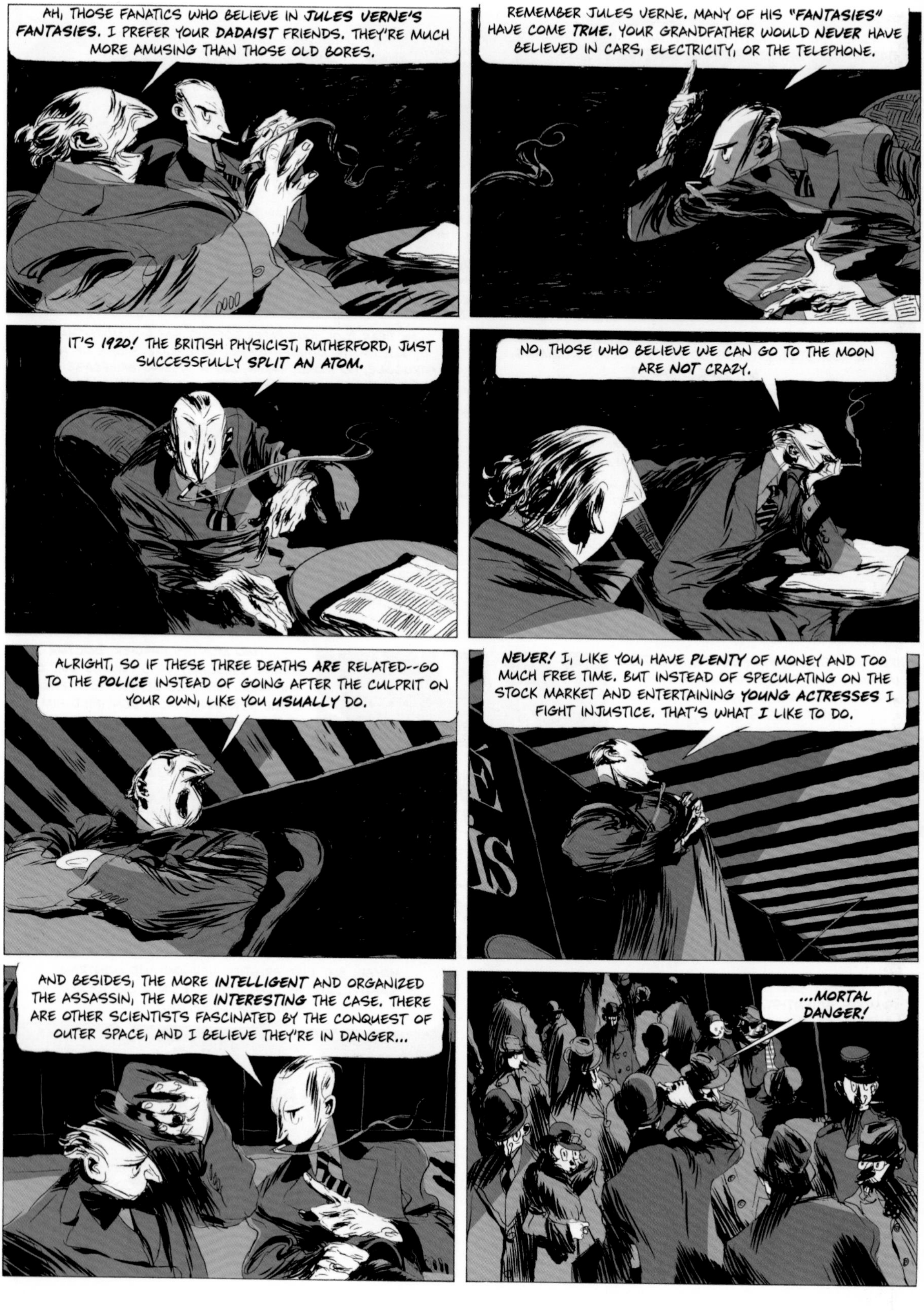
AH, THOSE FANATICS WHO BELIEVE IN JULES VERNE'S FANTASIES. I PREFER YOUR DADAIST FRIENDS. THEY'RE MUCH MORE AMUSING THAN THOSE OLD BORES.
REMEMBER JULES VERNE. MANY OF HIS "FANTASIES" HAVE COME TRUE. YOUR GRANDFATHER WOULD NEVER HAVE BELIEVED IN CARS, ELECTRICITY, OR THE TELEPHONE.
IT'S 1920! THE BRITISH PHYSICIST, RUTHERFORD, JUST SUCCESSFULLY SPLIT AN ATOM.
NO, THOSE WHO BELIEVE WE CAN GO TO THE MOON ARE NOT CRAZY.
ALRIGHT, SO IF THESE THREE DEATHS ARE RELATED--GO TO THE POLICE INSTEAD OF GOING AFTER THE CULPRIT ON YOUR OWN, LIKE YOU USUALLY DO.
NEVER! I, LIKE YOU, HAVE PLENTY OF MONEY AND TOO MUCH FREE TIME. BUT INSTEAD OF SPECULATING ON THE STOCK MARKET AND ENTERTAINING YOUNG ACTRESSES I FIGHT INJUSTICE. THAT'S WHAT I LIKE TO DO.
AND BESIDES, THE MORE INTELLIGENT AND ORGANIZED THE ASSASSIN, THE MORE INTERESTING THE CASE. THERE ARE OTHER SCIENTISTS FASCINATED BY THE CONQUEST OF OUTER SPACE, AND I BELIEVE THEY'RE IN DANGER...
...MORTAL DANGER!

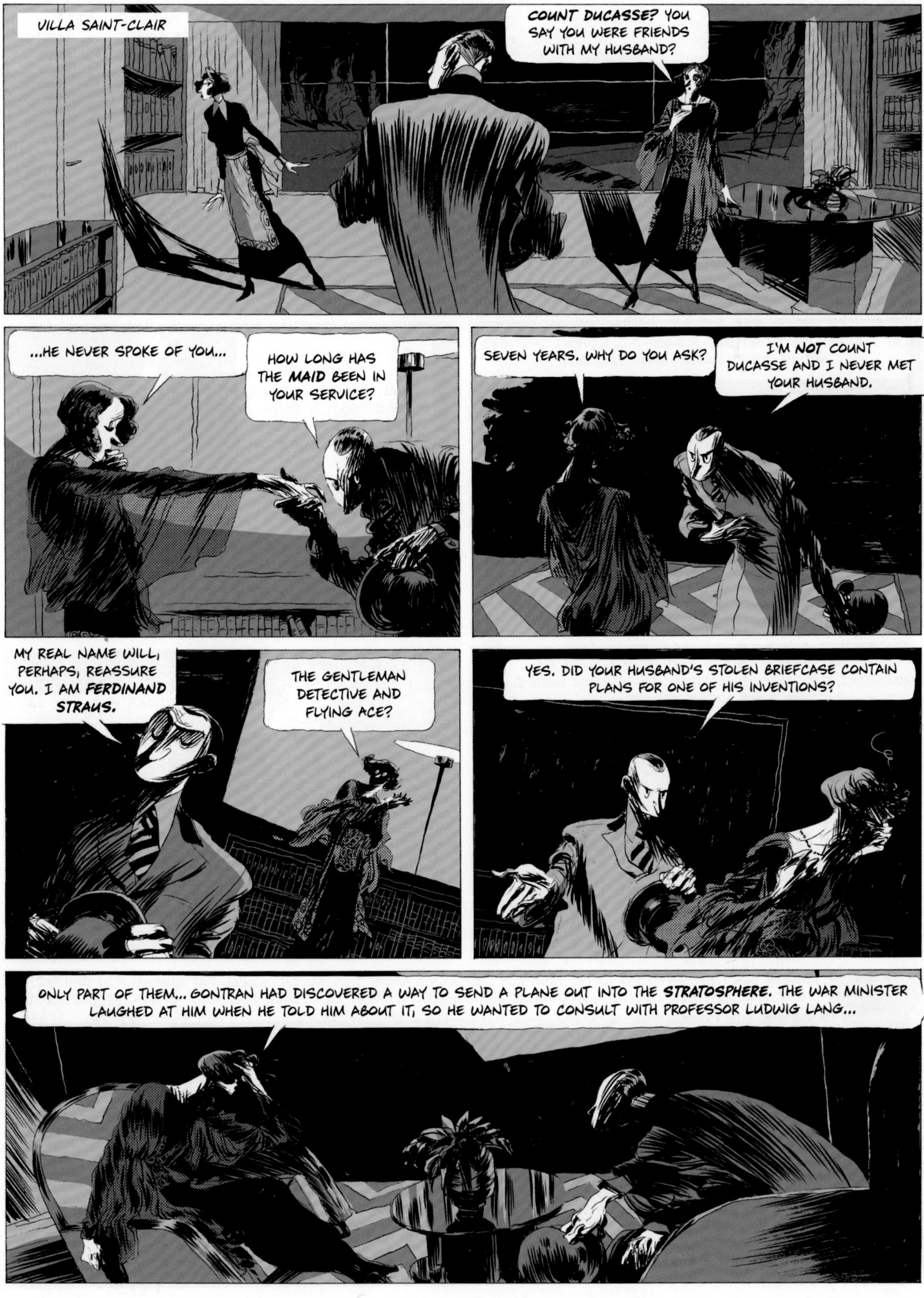
VILLA SAINT-CLAIR
COUNT DUCASSE? YOU SAY YOU WERE FRIENDS WITH MY HUSBAND?
...HE NEVER SPOKE OF YOU...
HOW LONG HAS THE MAID BEEN IN YOUR SERVICE?
SEVEN YEARS. WHY DO YOU ASK?
I'M NOT COUNT DUCASSE AND I NEVER MET YOUR HUSBAND.
MY REAL NAME WILL, PERHAPS, REASSURE YOU. I AM FERDINAND STRAUS.
THE GENTLEMAN DETECTIVE AND FLYING ACE?
YES. DID YOUR HUSBAND'S STOLEN BRIEFCASE CONTAIN PLANS FOR ONE OF HIS INVENTIONS?
ONLY PART OF THEM... GONTRAN HAD DISCOVERED A WAY TO SEND A PLANE OUT INTO THE STRATOSPHERE. THE WAR MINISTER LAUGHED AT HIM WHEN HE TOLD HIM ABOUT IT, SO HE WANTED TO CONSULT WITH PROFESSOR LUDWIG LANG...

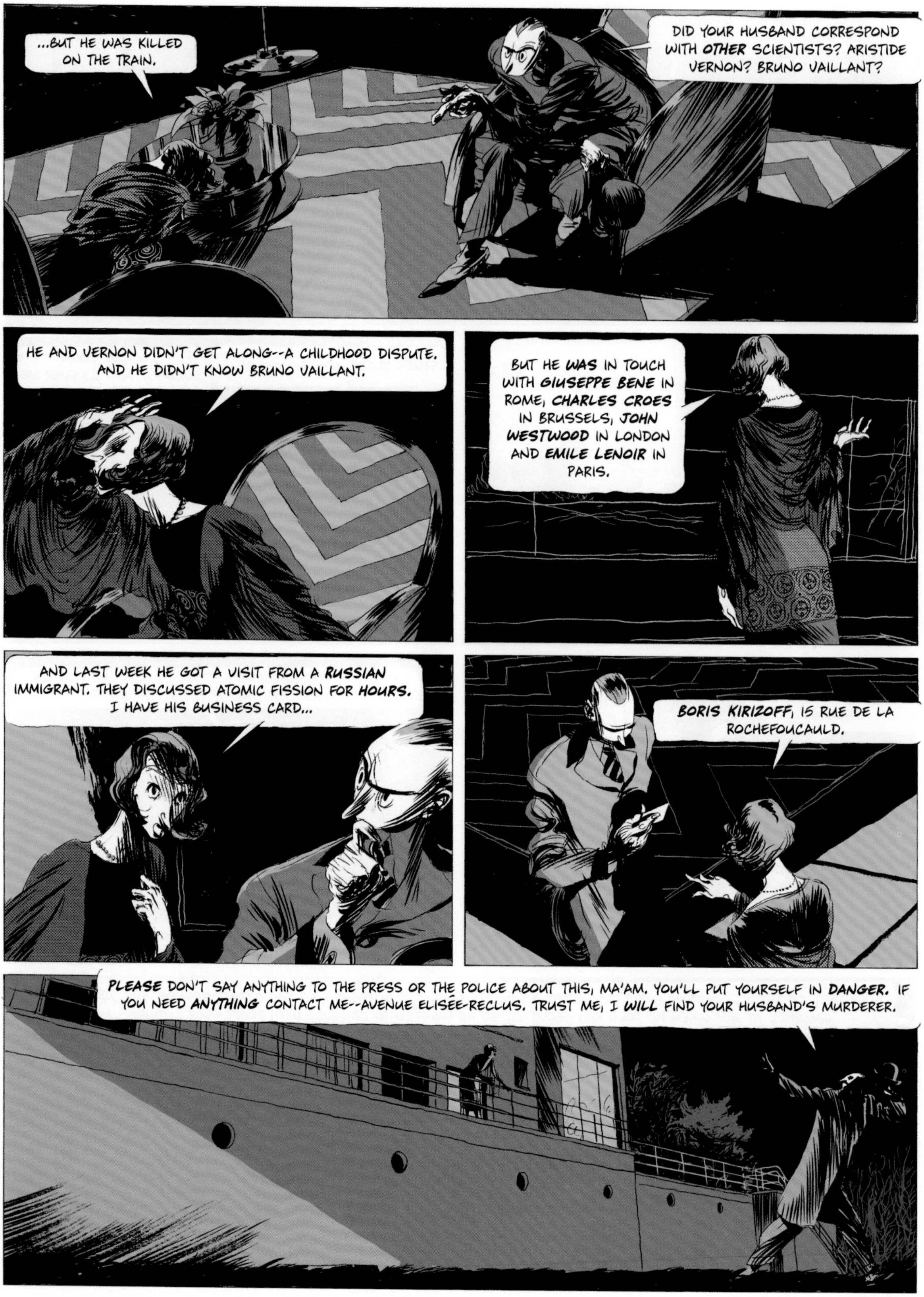
...BUT HE WAS KILLED ON THE TRAIN.
DID YOUR HUSBAND CORRESPOND WITH **OTHER** SCIENTISTS? ARISTIDE VERNON? BRUNO VAILLANT?
HE AND VERNON DIDN'T GET ALONG--A CHILDHOOD DISPUTE. AND HE DIDN'T KNOW BRUNO VAILLANT.
BUT HE **WAS** IN TOUCH WITH **GIUSEPPE BENE** IN ROME, **CHARLES CROES** IN BRUSSELS, **JOHN WESTWOOD** IN LONDON AND **EMILE LENOIR** IN PARIS.
AND LAST WEEK HE GOT A VISIT FROM A **RUSSIAN** IMMIGRANT. THEY DISCUSSED ATOMIC FISSION FOR **HOURS.** I HAVE HIS BUSINESS CARD...
BORIS KIRIZOFF, 15 RUE DE LA ROCHEFOUCAULD.
PLEASE DON'T SAY ANYTHING TO THE PRESS OR THE POLICE ABOUT THIS, MA'AM. YOU'LL PUT YOURSELF IN **DANGER.** IF YOU NEED **ANYTHING** CONTACT ME--AVENUE ELISÉE-RECLUS. TRUST ME, I **WILL** FIND YOUR HUSBAND'S MURDERER.

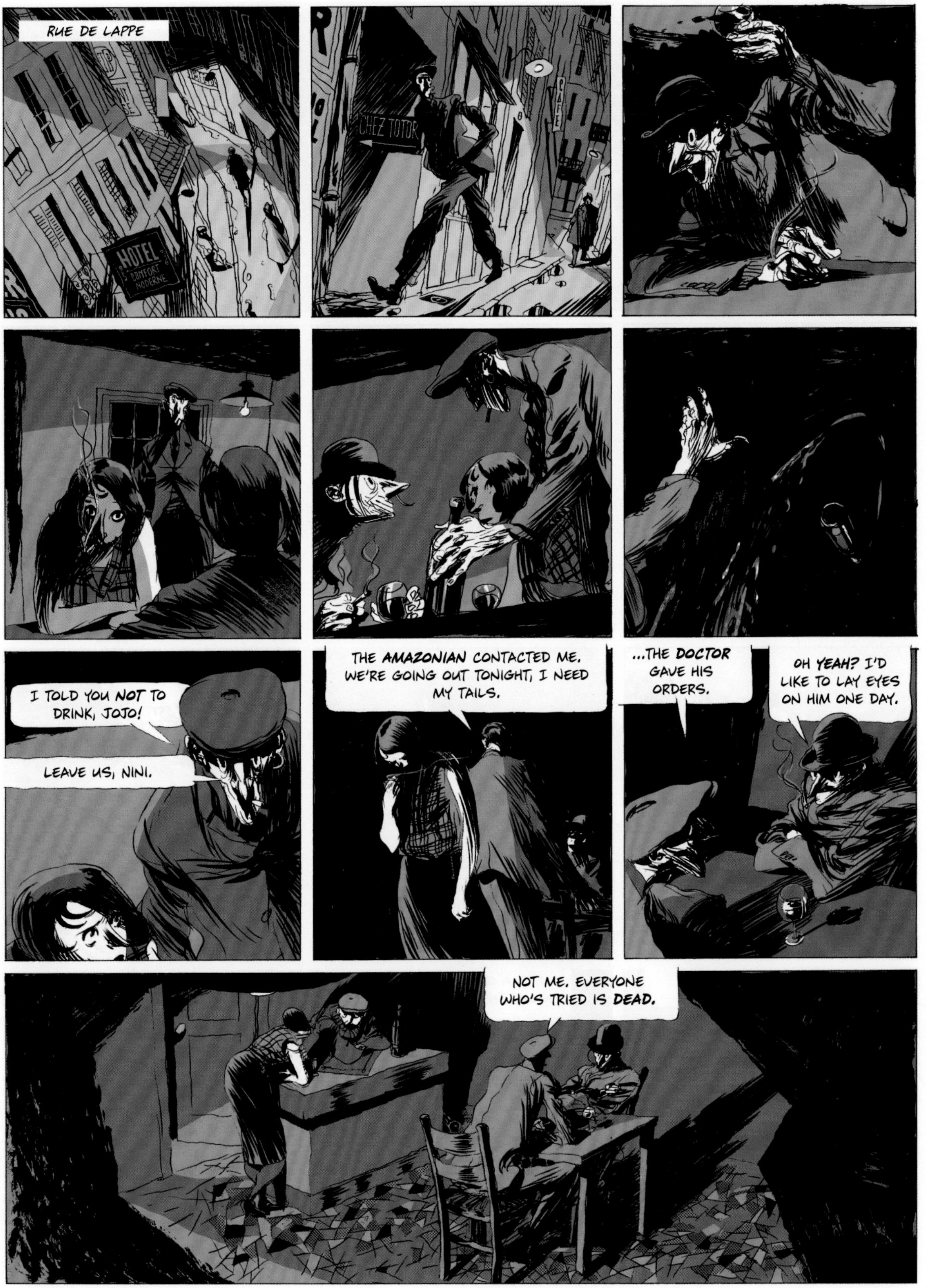
RUE DE LAPPE
CHEZ TOTOR
HOTEL CONFORT MODERNE
I TOLD YOU NOT TO DRINK, JOJO!
LEAVE US, NINI.
THE AMAZONIAN CONTACTED ME. WE'RE GOING OUT TONIGHT, I NEED MY TAILS.
...THE DOCTOR GAVE HIS ORDERS.
OH YEAH? I'D LIKE TO LAY EYES ON HIM ONE DAY.
NOT ME. EVERYONE WHO'S TRIED IS DEAD.

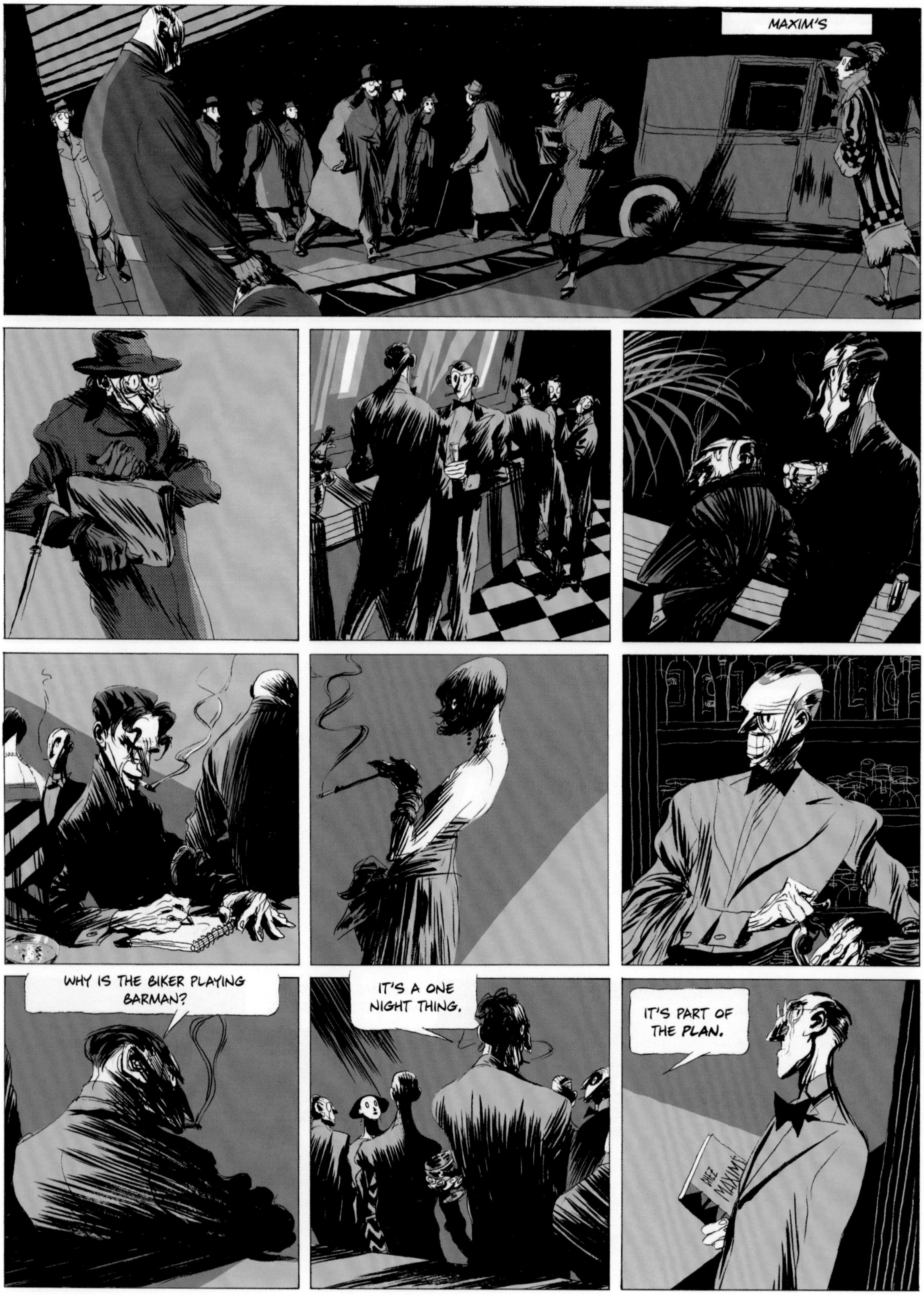
MAXIM'S
WHY IS THE BIKER PLAYING BARMAN?
IT'S A ONE NIGHT THING.
IT'S PART OF THE PLAN.
CHEZ MAXIM'S

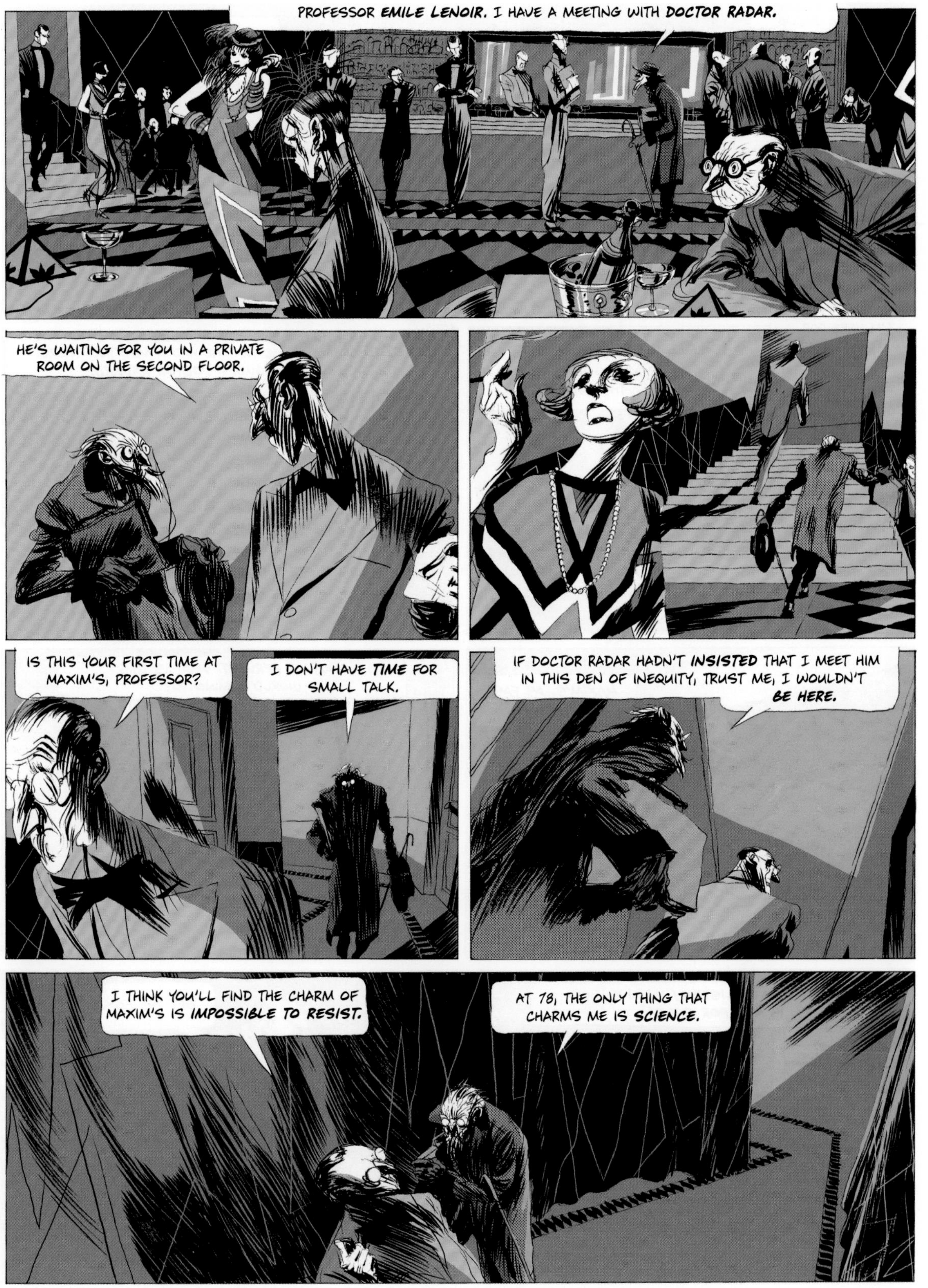
PROFESSOR EMILE LENOIR. I HAVE A MEETING WITH DOCTOR RADAR.
HE'S WAITING FOR YOU IN A PRIVATE ROOM ON THE SECOND FLOOR.
IS THIS YOUR FIRST TIME AT MAXIM'S, PROFESSOR?
I DON'T HAVE TIME FOR SMALL TALK.
IF DOCTOR RADAR HADN'T INSISTED THAT I MEET HIM IN THIS DEN OF INEQUITY, TRUST ME, I WOULDN'T BE HERE.
I THINK YOU'LL FIND THE CHARM OF MAXIM'S IS IMPOSSIBLE TO RESIST.
AT 78, THE ONLY THING THAT CHARMS ME IS SCIENCE.

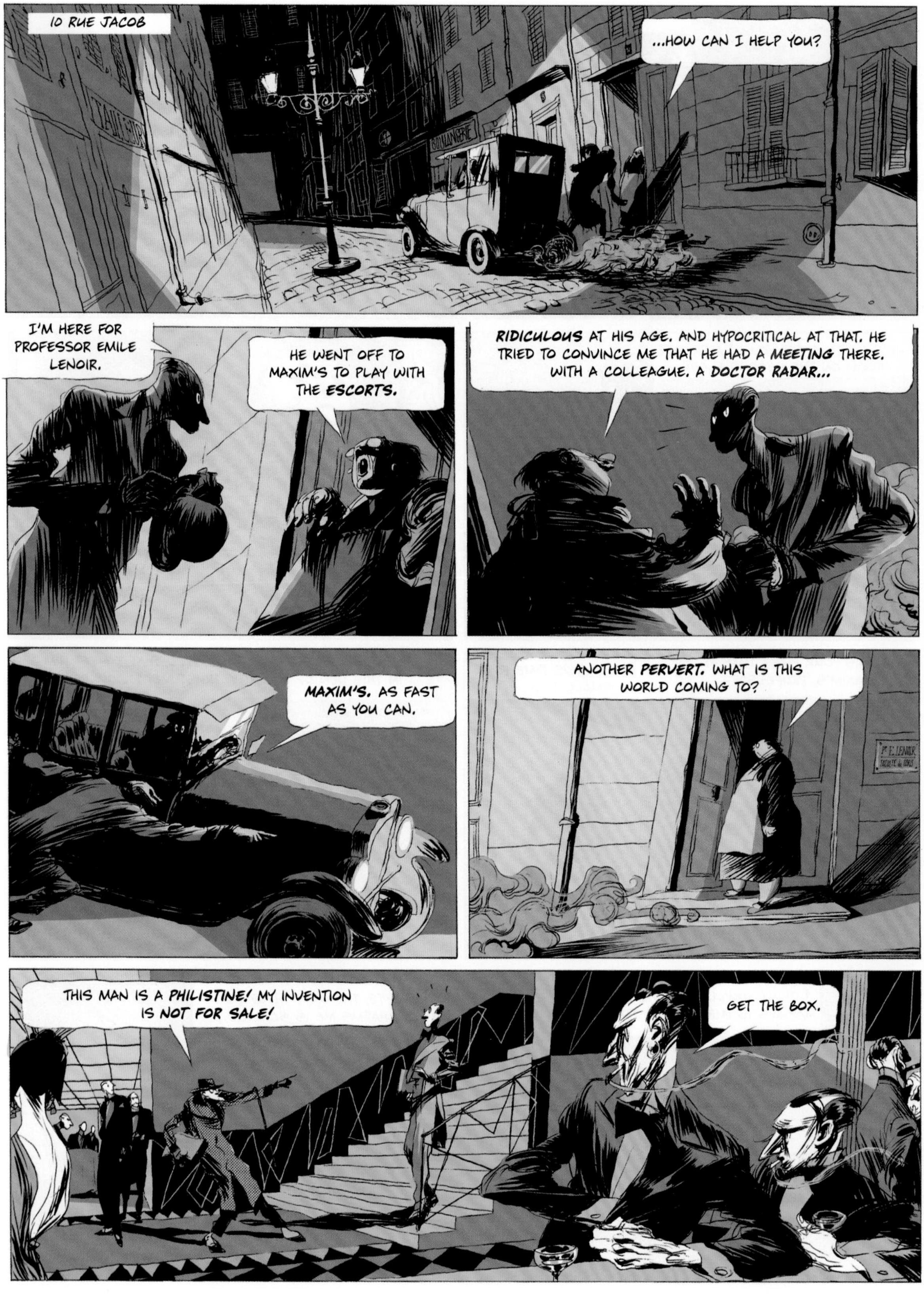
10 RUE JACOB
...HOW CAN I HELP YOU?
I'M HERE FOR PROFESSOR EMILE LENOIR.
HE WENT OFF TO MAXIM'S TO PLAY WITH THE ESCORTS.
RIDICULOUS AT HIS AGE. AND HYPOCRITICAL AT THAT. HE TRIED TO CONVINCE ME THAT HE HAD A MEETING THERE. WITH A COLLEAGUE. A DOCTOR RADAR...
MAXIM'S. AS FAST AS YOU CAN.
ANOTHER PERVERT. WHAT IS THIS WORLD COMING TO?
THIS MAN IS A PHILISTINE! MY INVENTION IS NOT FOR SALE!
GET THE BOX.

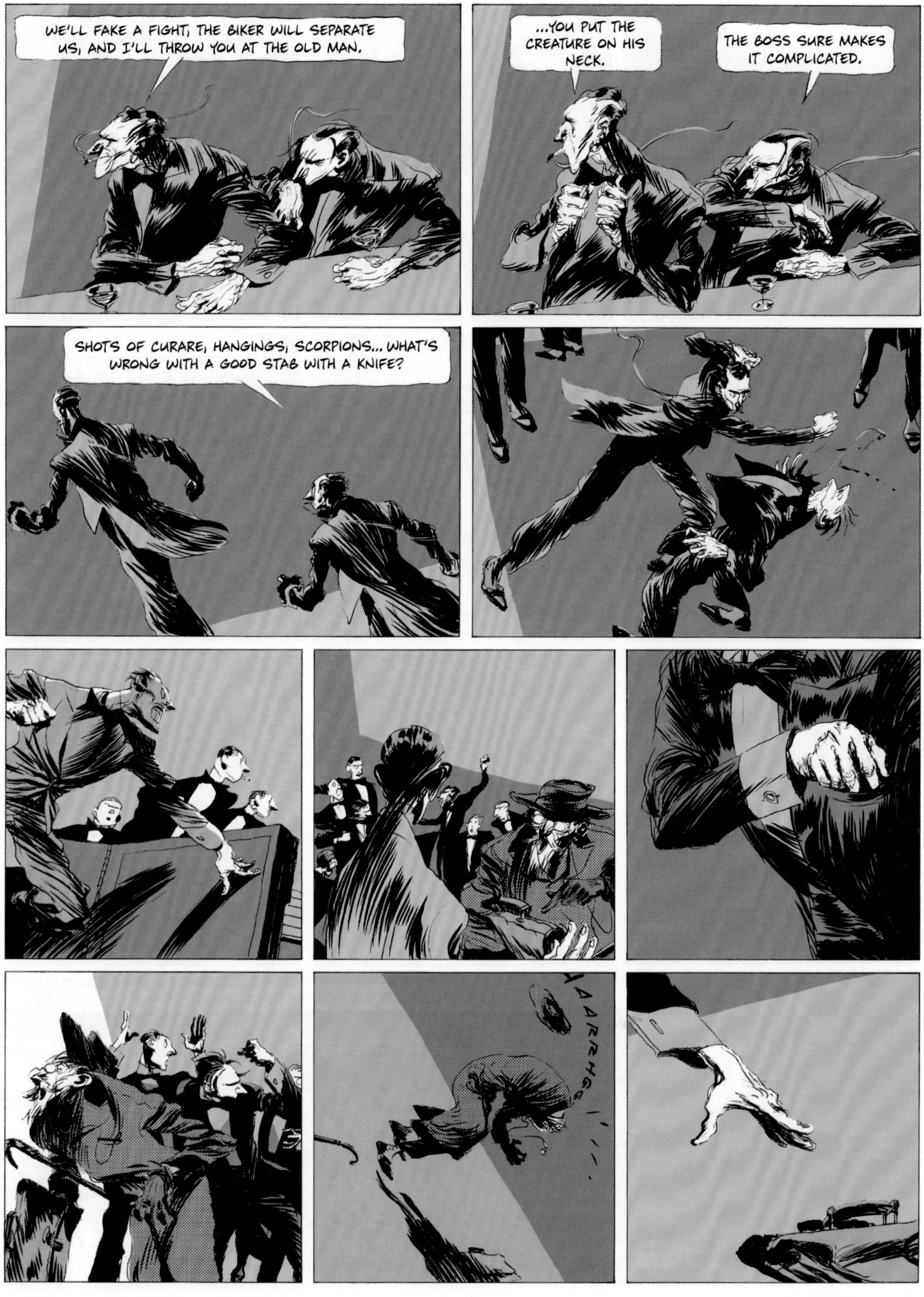
WE'LL FAKE A FIGHT, THE BIKER WILL SEPARATE US, AND I'LL THROW YOU AT THE OLD MAN.
...YOU PUT THE CREATURE ON HIS NECK.
THE BOSS SURE MAKES IT COMPLICATED.
SHOTS OF CURARE, HANGINGS, SCORPIONS... WHAT'S WRONG WITH A GOOD STAB WITH A KNIFE?
AAARRHGG!!!

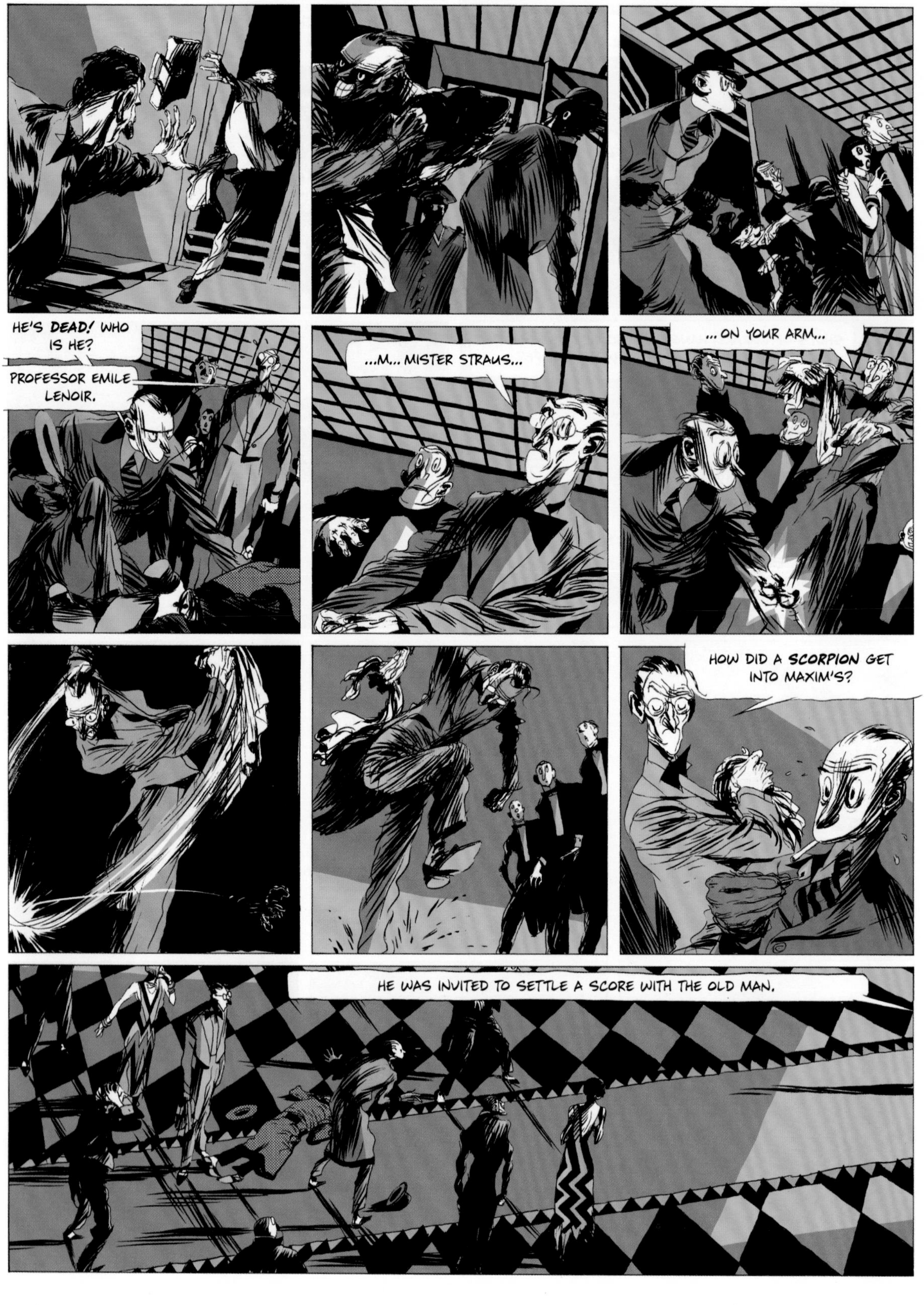
HE'S **DEAD!** WHO IS HE?
PROFESSOR EMILE LENOIR.
...M... MISTER STRAUS...
... ON YOUR ARM...
HOW DID A **SCORPION** GET INTO MAXIM'S?
HE WAS INVITED TO SETTLE A SCORE WITH THE OLD MAN.

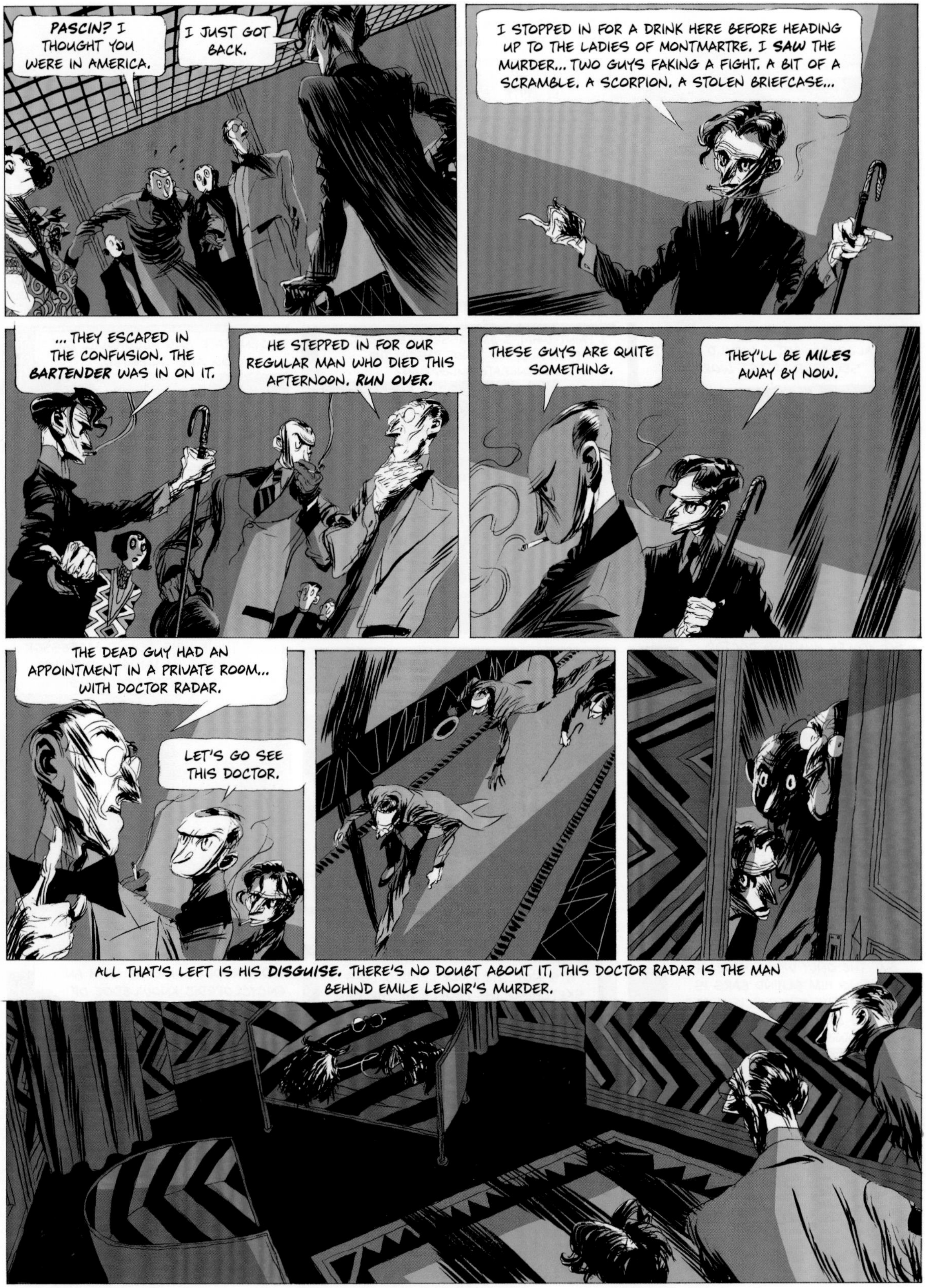
PASCIN? I THOUGHT YOU WERE IN AMERICA.
I JUST GOT BACK.
I STOPPED IN FOR A DRINK HERE BEFORE HEADING UP TO THE LADIES OF MONTMARTRE. I SAW THE MURDER... TWO GUYS FAKING A FIGHT. A BIT OF A SCRAMBLE. A SCORPION. A STOLEN BRIEFCASE...
... THEY ESCAPED IN THE CONFUSION. THE BARTENDER WAS IN ON IT.
HE STEPPED IN FOR OUR REGULAR MAN WHO DIED THIS AFTERNOON. RUN OVER.
THESE GUYS ARE QUITE SOMETHING.
THEY'LL BE MILES AWAY BY NOW.
THE DEAD GUY HAD AN APPOINTMENT IN A PRIVATE ROOM... WITH DOCTOR RADAR.
LET'S GO SEE THIS DOCTOR.
ALL THAT'S LEFT IS HIS DISGUISE. THERE'S NO DOUBT ABOUT IT, THIS DOCTOR RADAR IS THE MAN BEHIND EMILE LENOIR'S MURDER.

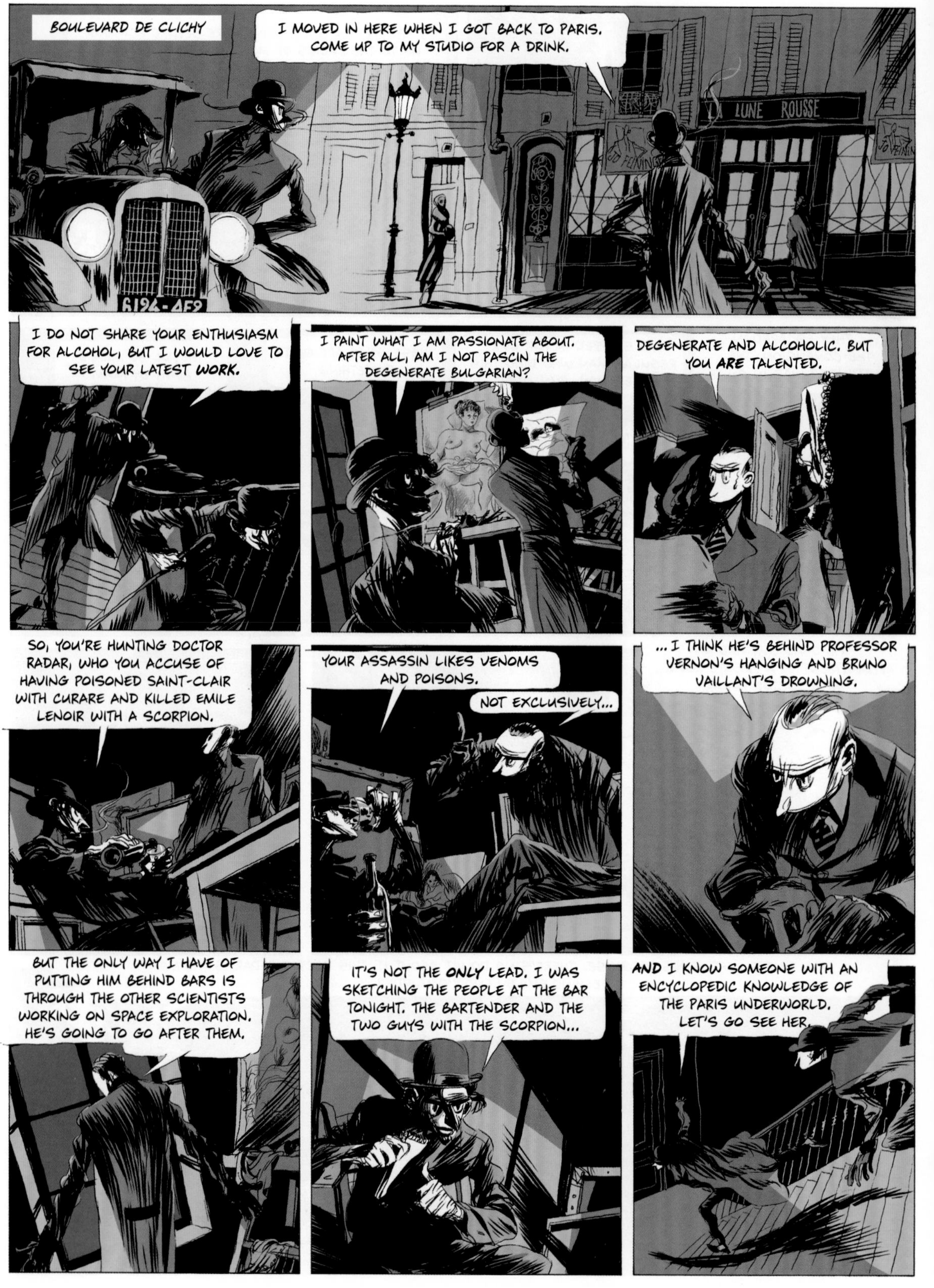
BOULEVARD DE CLICHY
I MOVED IN HERE WHEN I GOT BACK TO PARIS. COME UP TO MY STUDIO FOR A DRINK.
LA LUNE ROUSSE
I DO NOT SHARE YOUR ENTHUSIASM FOR ALCOHOL, BUT I WOULD LOVE TO SEE YOUR LATEST **WORK.**
I PAINT WHAT I AM PASSIONATE ABOUT. AFTER ALL, AM I NOT PASCIN THE DEGENERATE BULGARIAN?
DEGENERATE AND ALCOHOLIC. BUT YOU **ARE** TALENTED.
SO, YOU'RE HUNTING DOCTOR RADAR, WHO YOU ACCUSE OF HAVING POISONED SAINT-CLAIR WITH CURARE AND KILLED EMILE LENOIR WITH A SCORPION.
YOUR ASSASSIN LIKES VENOMS AND POISONS.
NOT EXCLUSIVELY...
... I THINK HE'S BEHIND PROFESSOR VERNON'S HANGING AND BRUNO VAILLANT'S DROWNING.
BUT THE ONLY WAY I HAVE OF PUTTING HIM BEHIND BARS IS THROUGH THE OTHER SCIENTISTS WORKING ON SPACE EXPLORATION. HE'S GOING TO GO AFTER THEM.
IT'S NOT THE **ONLY** LEAD. I WAS SKETCHING THE PEOPLE AT THE BAR TONIGHT. THE BARTENDER AND THE TWO GUYS WITH THE SCORPION...
AND I KNOW SOMEONE WITH AN ENCYCLOPEDIC KNOWLEDGE OF THE PARIS UNDERWORLD. LET'S GO SEE HER.

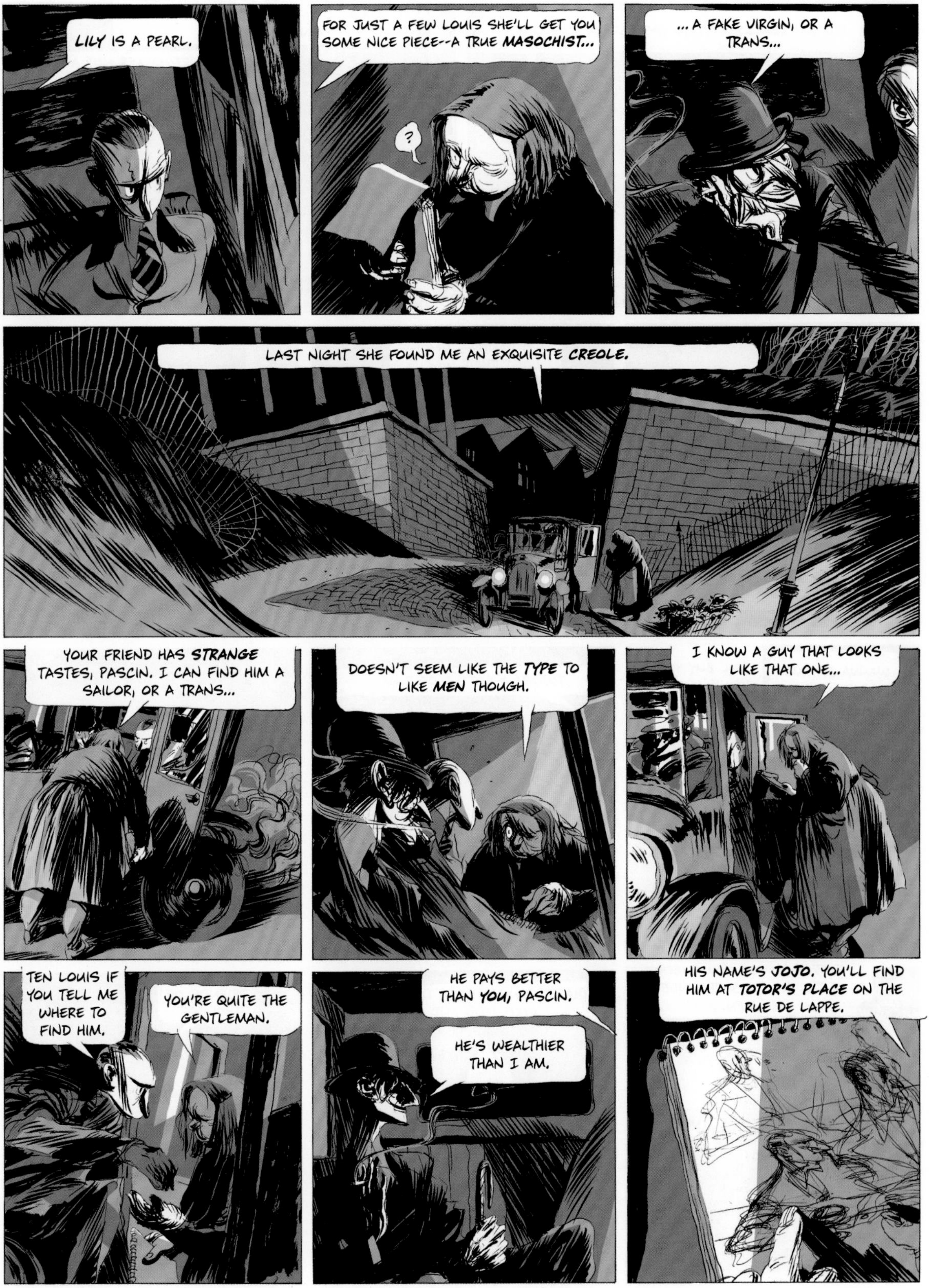
LILY IS A PEARL.
FOR JUST A FEW LOUIS SHE'LL GET YOU SOME NICE PIECE--A TRUE MASOCHIST...
?
...A FAKE VIRGIN, OR A TRANS...
LAST NIGHT SHE FOUND ME AN EXQUISITE CREOLE.
YOUR FRIEND HAS STRANGE TASTES, PASCIN. I CAN FIND HIM A SAILOR, OR A TRANS...
DOESN'T SEEM LIKE THE TYPE TO LIKE MEN THOUGH.
I KNOW A GUY THAT LOOKS LIKE THAT ONE...
TEN LOUIS IF YOU TELL ME WHERE TO FIND HIM.
YOU'RE QUITE THE GENTLEMAN.
HE PAYS BETTER THAN YOU, PASCIN.
HE'S WEALTHIER THAN I AM.
HIS NAME'S JOJO. YOU'LL FIND HIM AT TOTOR'S PLACE ON THE RUE DE LAPPE.

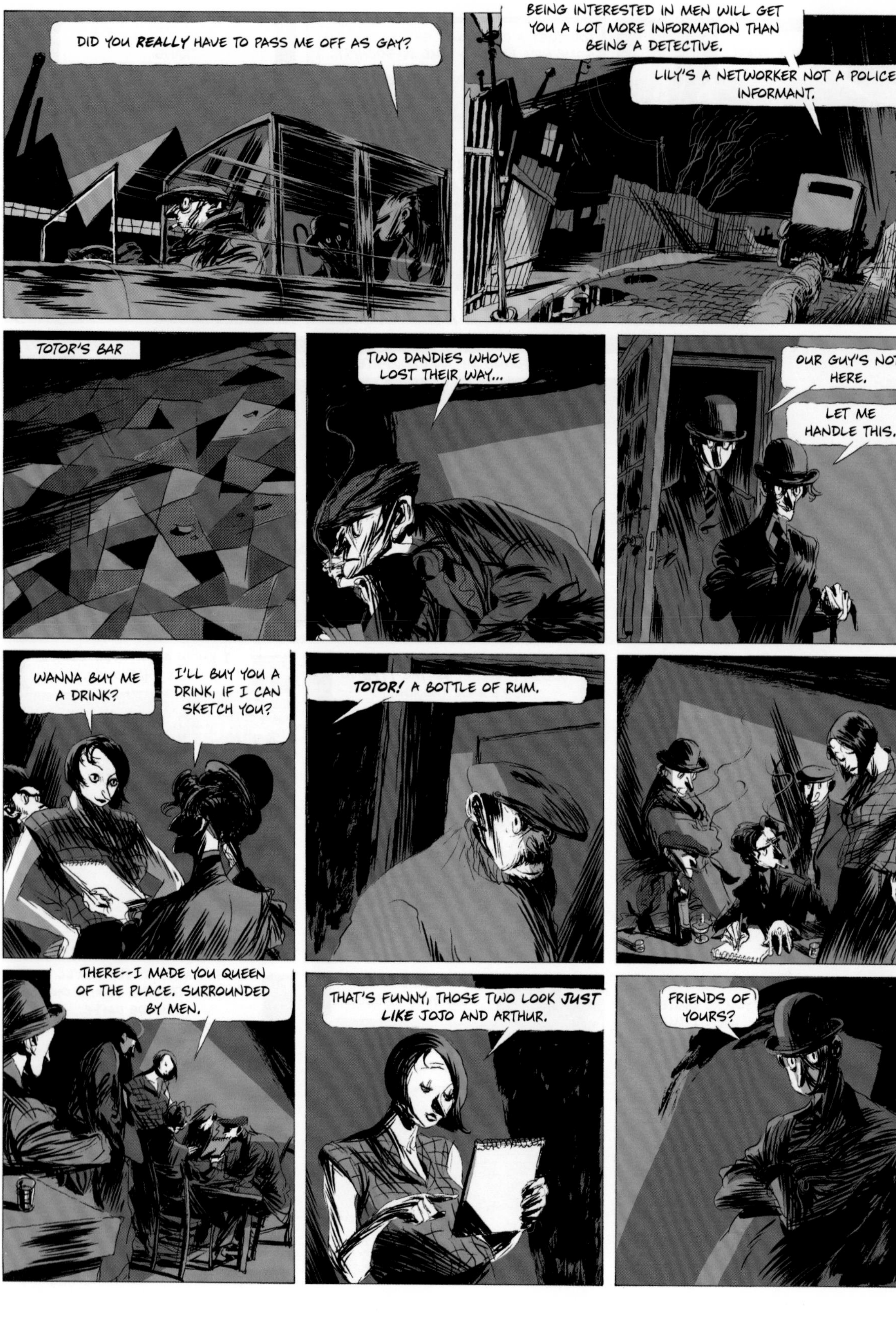
DID YOU **REALLY** HAVE TO PASS ME OFF AS GAY?
BEING INTERESTED IN MEN WILL GET YOU A LOT MORE INFORMATION THAN BEING A DETECTIVE.
LILY'S A NETWORKER NOT A POLICE INFORMANT.
TOTOR'S BAR
TWO DANDIES WHO'VE LOST THEIR WAY...
OUR GUY'S NOT HERE.
LET ME HANDLE THIS.
WANNA BUY ME A DRINK?
I'LL BUY YOU A DRINK, IF I CAN SKETCH YOU?
TOTOR! A BOTTLE OF RUM.
THERE--I MADE YOU QUEEN OF THE PLACE. SURROUNDED BY MEN.
THAT'S FUNNY, THOSE TWO LOOK **JUST LIKE** JOJO AND ARTHUR.
FRIENDS OF YOURS?

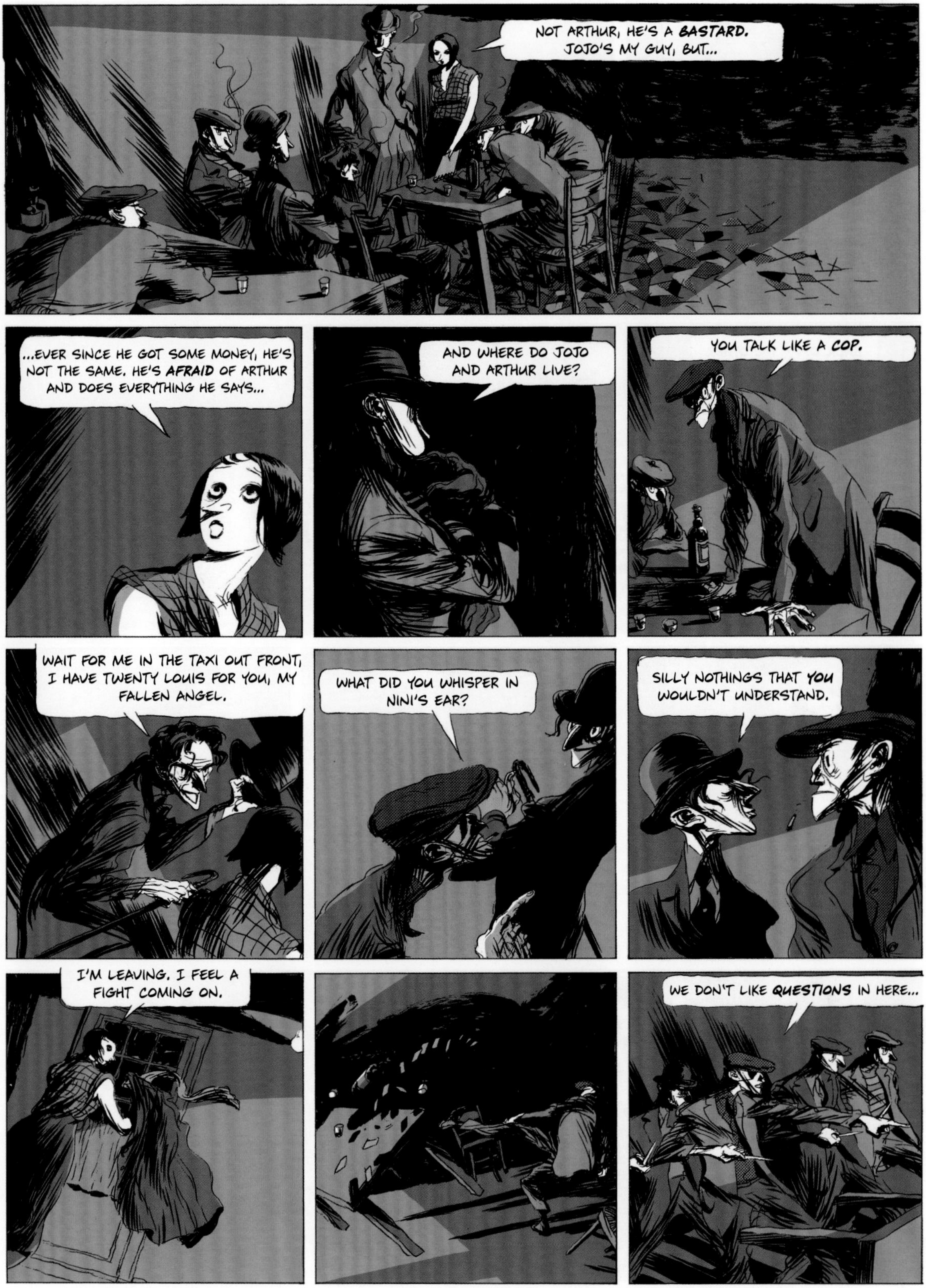
NOT ARTHUR, HE'S A **BASTARD.** JOJO'S MY GUY, BUT...
...EVER SINCE HE GOT SOME MONEY, HE'S NOT THE SAME. HE'S ***AFRAID*** OF ARTHUR AND DOES EVERYTHING HE SAYS...
AND WHERE DO JOJO AND ARTHUR LIVE?
YOU TALK LIKE A **COP.**
WAIT FOR ME IN THE TAXI OUT FRONT, I HAVE TWENTY LOUIS FOR YOU, MY FALLEN ANGEL.
WHAT DID YOU WHISPER IN NINI'S EAR?
SILLY NOTHINGS THAT **YOU** WOULDN'T UNDERSTAND.
I'M LEAVING. I FEEL A FIGHT COMING ON.
WE DON'T LIKE **QUESTIONS** IN HERE...

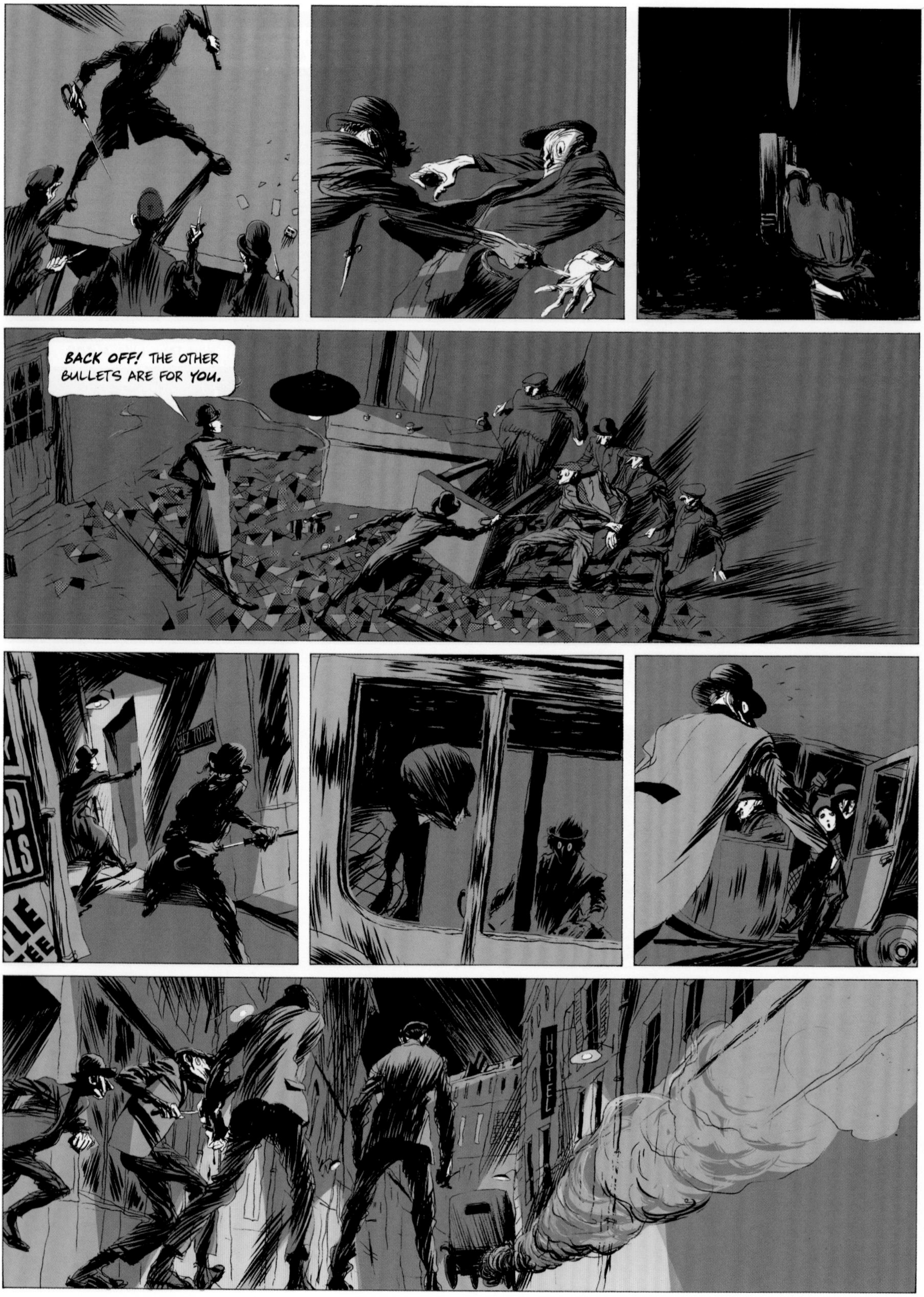
BACK OFF! THE OTHER BULLETS ARE FOR YOU.
CHEZ TOTOR
HOTEL

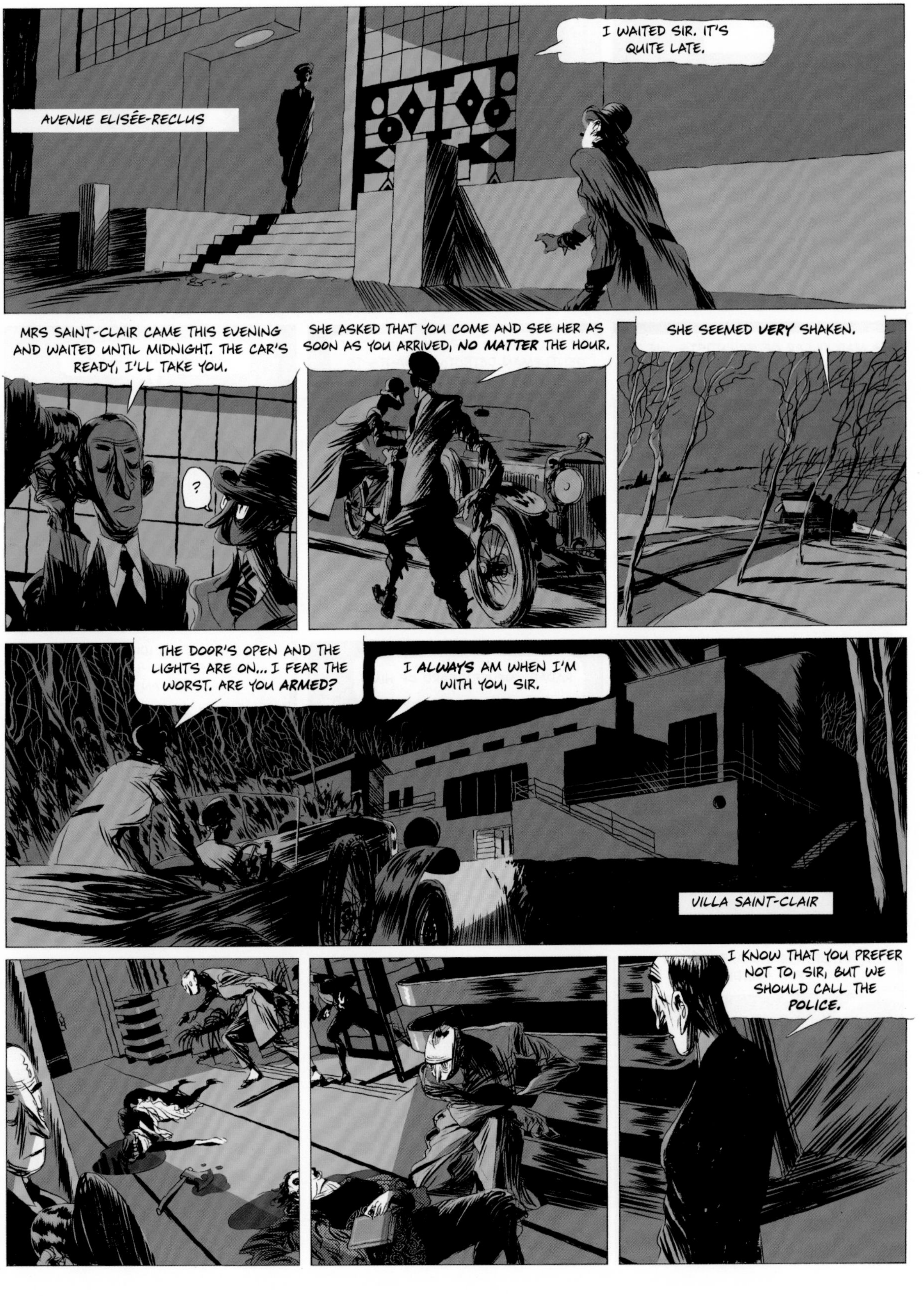
AVENUE ELISÉE-RECLUS
I WAITED SIR. IT'S QUITE LATE.
MRS SAINT-CLAIR CAME THIS EVENING AND WAITED UNTIL MIDNIGHT. THE CAR'S READY, I'LL TAKE YOU.
?
SHE ASKED THAT YOU COME AND SEE HER AS SOON AS YOU ARRIVED, **NO MATTER** THE HOUR.
SHE SEEMED **VERY** SHAKEN.
THE DOOR'S OPEN AND THE LIGHTS ARE ON... I FEAR THE WORST. ARE YOU **ARMED?**
I **ALWAYS** AM WHEN I'M WITH YOU, SIR.
VILLA SAINT-CLAIR
I KNOW THAT YOU PREFER NOT TO, SIR, BUT WE SHOULD CALL THE **POLICE.**

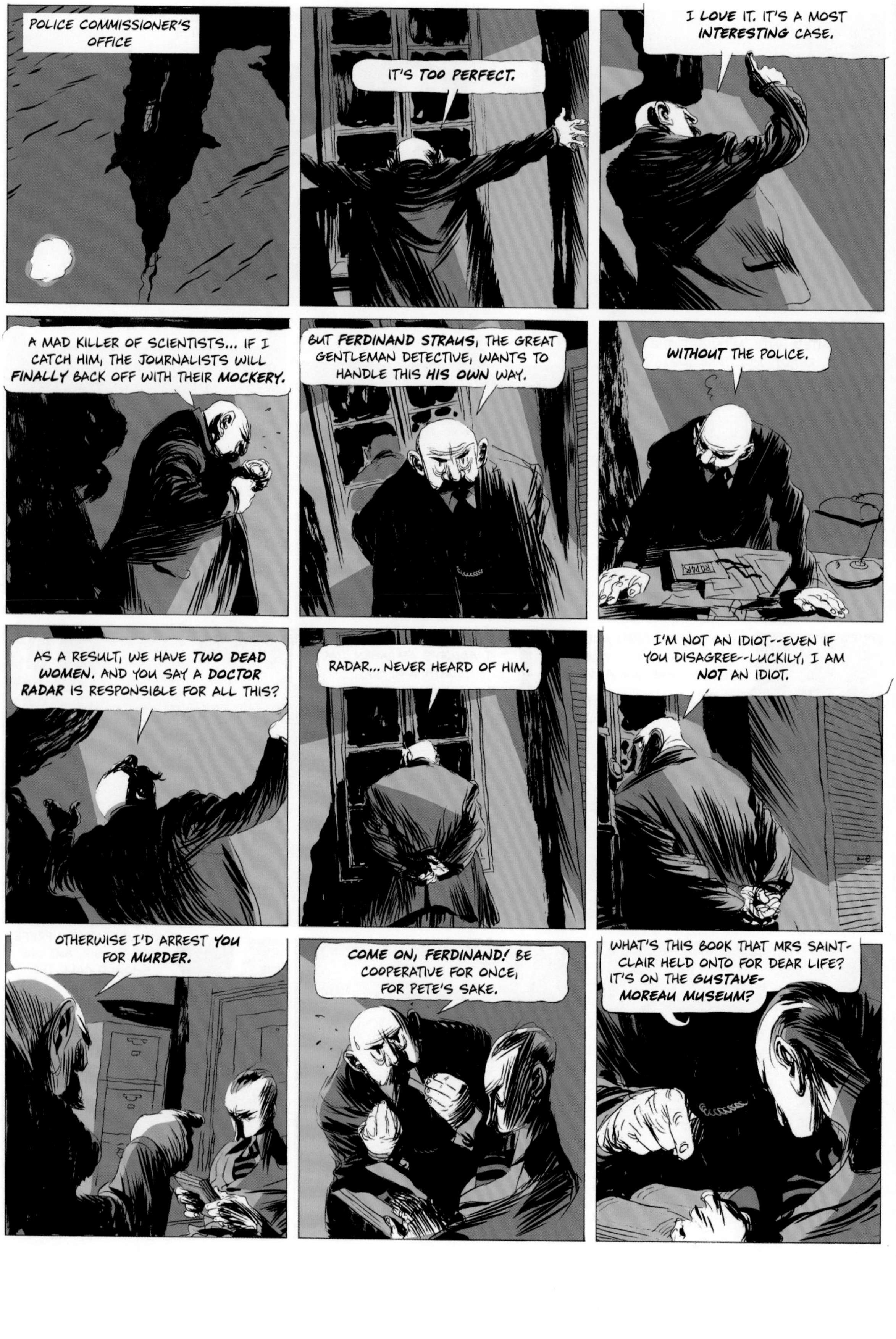
POLICE COMMISSIONER'S OFFICE
IT'S TOO PERFECT.
I LOVE IT. IT'S A MOST INTERESTING CASE.
A MAD KILLER OF SCIENTISTS... IF I CATCH HIM, THE JOURNALISTS WILL FINALLY BACK OFF WITH THEIR MOCKERY.
BUT FERDINAND STRAUS, THE GREAT GENTLEMAN DETECTIVE, WANTS TO HANDLE THIS HIS OWN WAY.
WITHOUT THE POLICE.
AS A RESULT, WE HAVE TWO DEAD WOMEN. AND YOU SAY A DOCTOR RADAR IS RESPONSIBLE FOR ALL THIS?
RADAR... NEVER HEARD OF HIM.
I'M NOT AN IDIOT--EVEN IF YOU DISAGREE--LUCKILY, I AM NOT AN IDIOT.
OTHERWISE I'D ARREST YOU FOR MURDER.
COME ON, FERDINAND! BE COOPERATIVE FOR ONCE, FOR PETE'S SAKE.
WHAT'S THIS BOOK THAT MRS SAINT-CLAIR HELD ONTO FOR DEAR LIFE? IT'S ON THE GUSTAVE-MOREAU MUSEUM?

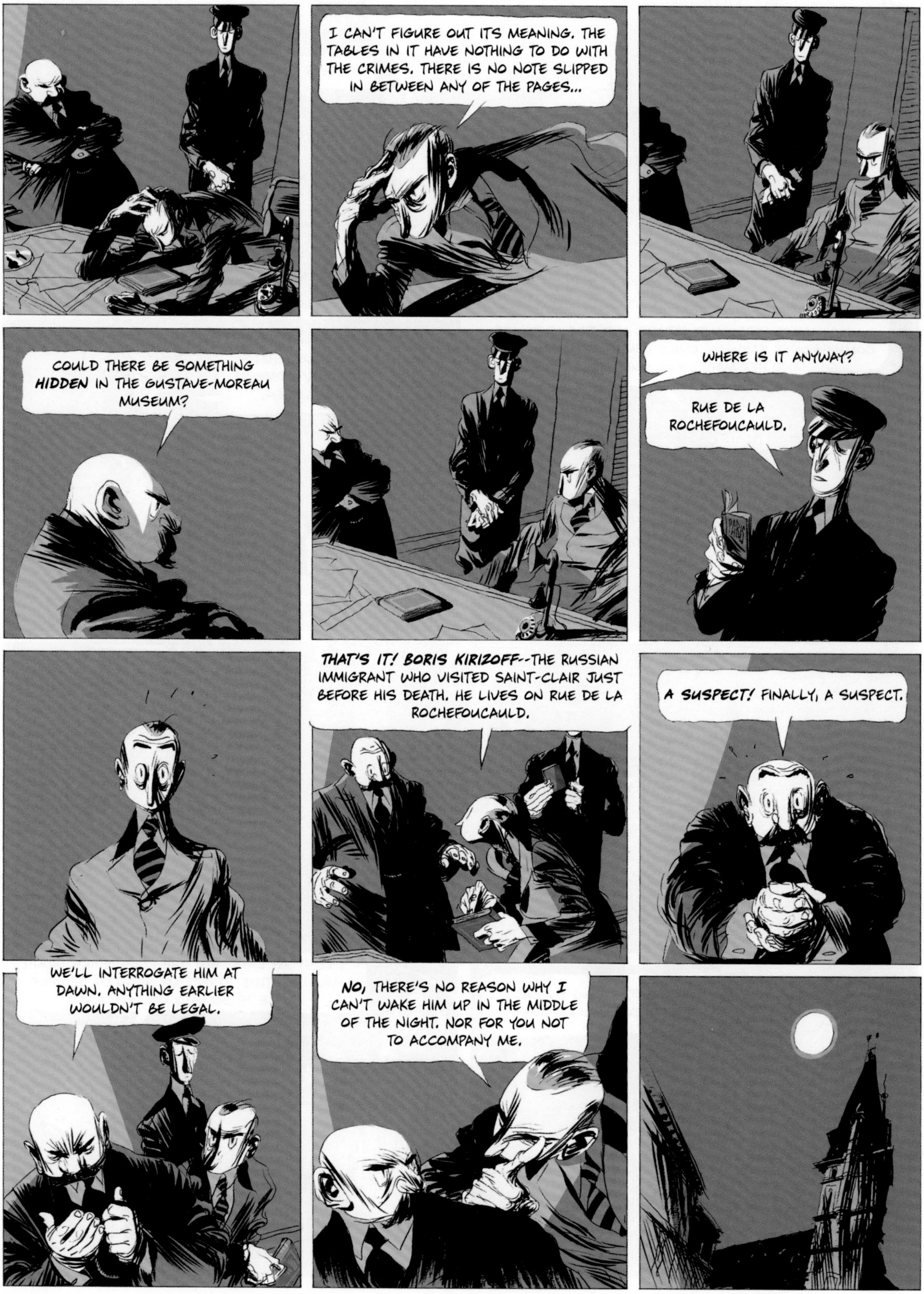
I CAN'T FIGURE OUT ITS MEANING. THE TABLES IN IT HAVE NOTHING TO DO WITH THE CRIMES. THERE IS NO NOTE SLIPPED IN BETWEEN ANY OF THE PAGES...
COULD THERE BE SOMETHING HIDDEN IN THE GUSTAVE-MOREAU MUSEUM?
WHERE IS IT ANYWAY?
RUE DE LA ROCHEFOUCAULD.
PARIS
THAT'S IT! BORIS KIRIZOFF--THE RUSSIAN IMMIGRANT WHO VISITED SAINT-CLAIR JUST BEFORE HIS DEATH. HE LIVES ON RUE DE LA ROCHEFOUCAULD.
A SUSPECT! FINALLY, A SUSPECT.
WE'LL INTERROGATE HIM AT DAWN. ANYTHING EARLIER WOULDN'T BE LEGAL.
NO, THERE'S NO REASON WHY I CAN'T WAKE HIM UP IN THE MIDDLE OF THE NIGHT. NOR FOR YOU NOT TO ACCOMPANY ME.

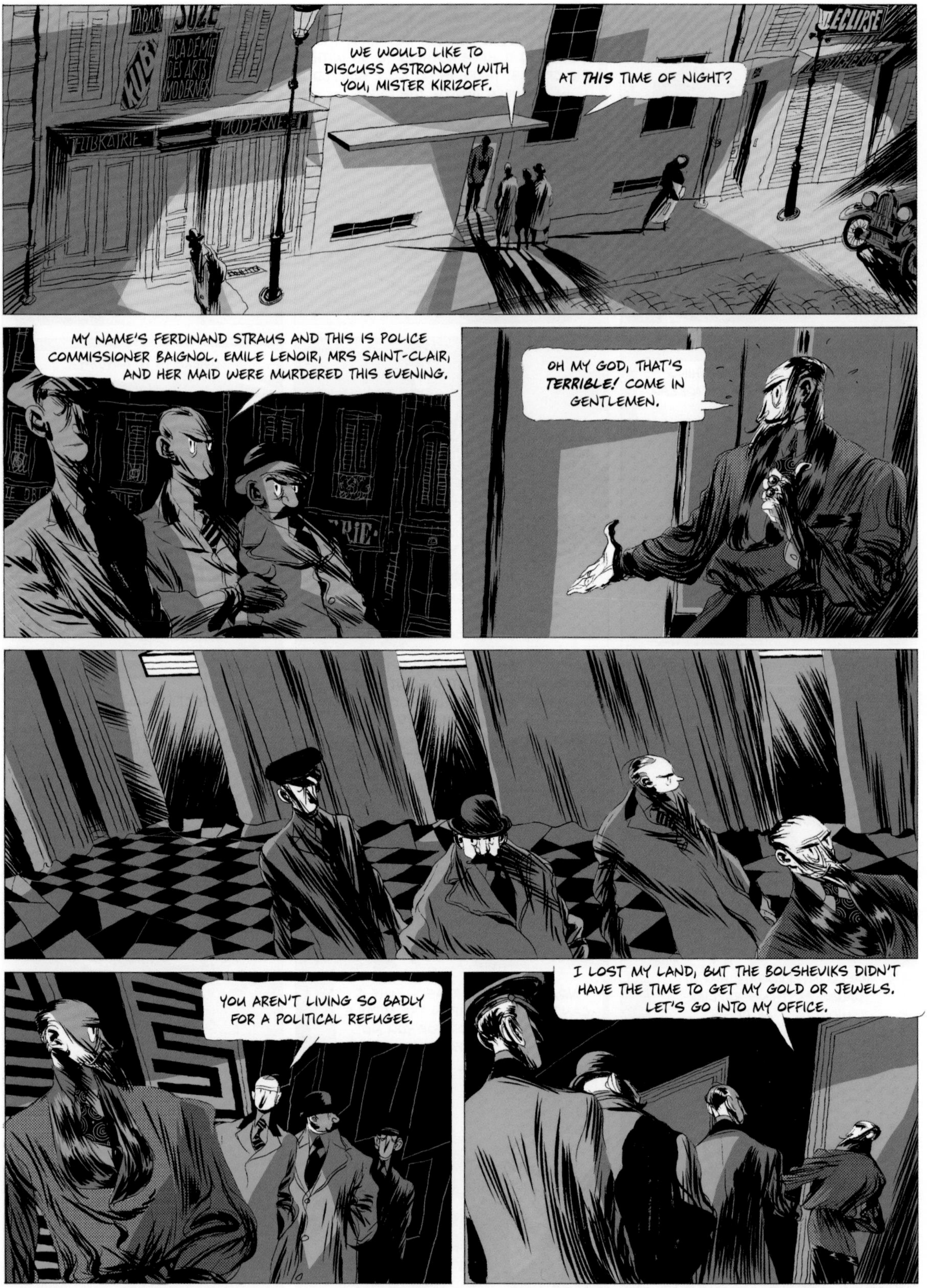
WE WOULD LIKE TO DISCUSS ASTRONOMY WITH YOU, MISTER KIRIZOFF.
AT **THIS** TIME OF NIGHT?
TABAC
SUZE
KUB
ACADÉMIE DES ARTS MODERNES
LIBRAIRIE
MODERNE
ECLIPSE
MY NAME'S FERDINAND STRAUS AND THIS IS POLICE COMMISSIONER BAIGNOL. EMILE LENOIR, MRS SAINT-CLAIR, AND HER MAID WERE MURDERED THIS EVENING.
OH MY GOD, THAT'S ***TERRIBLE!*** COME IN GENTLEMEN.
YOU AREN'T LIVING SO BADLY FOR A POLITICAL REFUGEE.
I LOST MY LAND, BUT THE BOLSHEVIKS DIDN'T HAVE THE TIME TO GET MY GOLD OR JEWELS. LET'S GO INTO MY OFFICE.

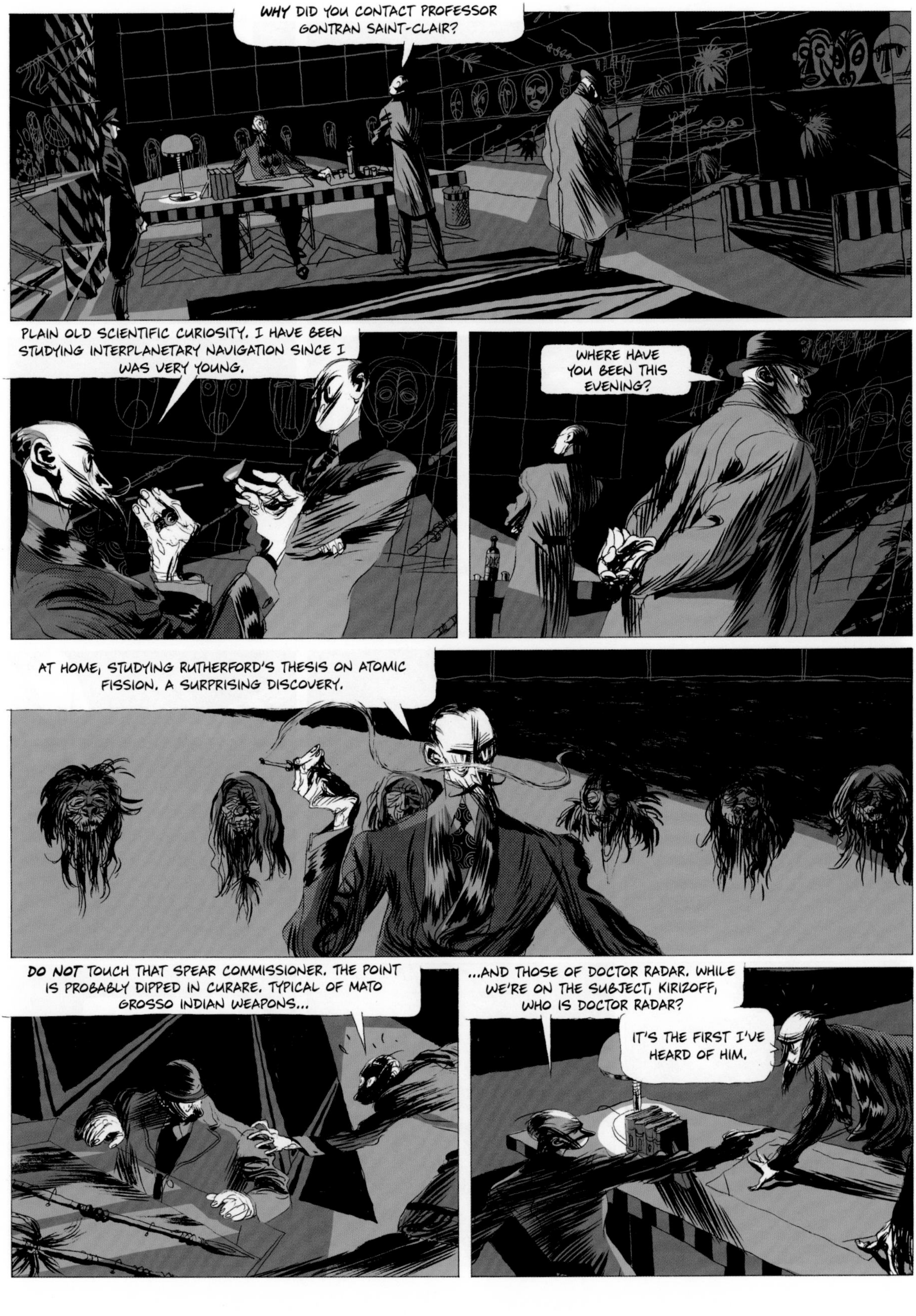
WHY DID YOU CONTACT PROFESSOR GONTRAN SAINT-CLAIR?
PLAIN OLD SCIENTIFIC CURIOSITY. I HAVE BEEN STUDYING INTERPLANETARY NAVIGATION SINCE I WAS VERY YOUNG.
WHERE HAVE YOU BEEN THIS EVENING?
AT HOME, STUDYING RUTHERFORD'S THESIS ON ATOMIC FISSION. A SURPRISING DISCOVERY.
DO NOT TOUCH THAT SPEAR COMMISSIONER. THE POINT IS PROBABLY DIPPED IN CURARE. TYPICAL OF MATO GROSSO INDIAN WEAPONS...
...AND THOSE OF DOCTOR RADAR. WHILE WE'RE ON THE SUBJECT, KIRIZOFF, WHO IS DOCTOR RADAR?
IT'S THE FIRST I'VE HEARD OF HIM.

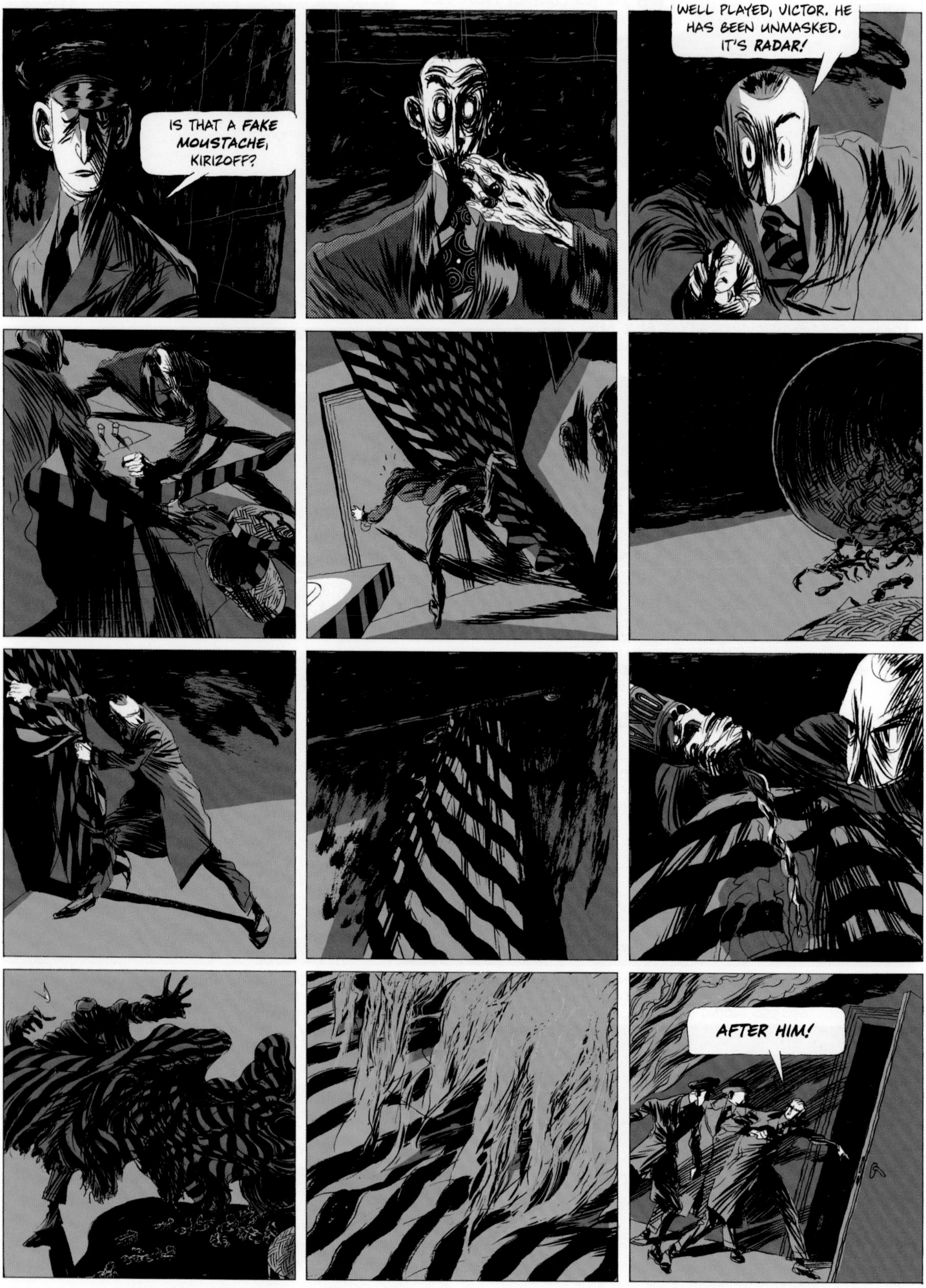
IS THAT A FAKE MOUSTACHE, KIRIZOFF?
WELL PLAYED, VICTOR. HE HAS BEEN UNMASKED. IT'S RADAR!
AFTER HIM!

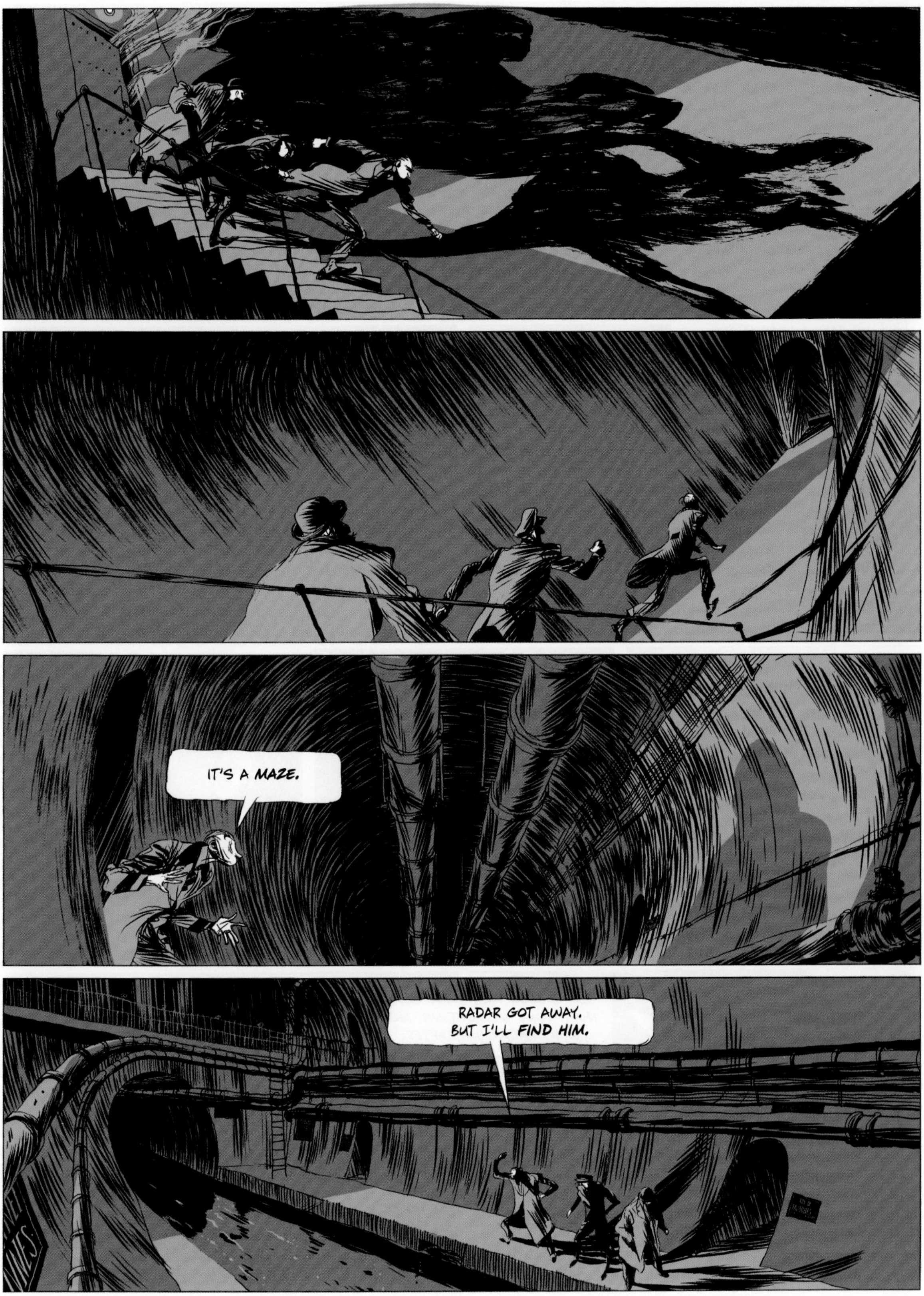
IT'S A MAZE.
RADAR GOT AWAY. BUT I'LL FIND HIM.

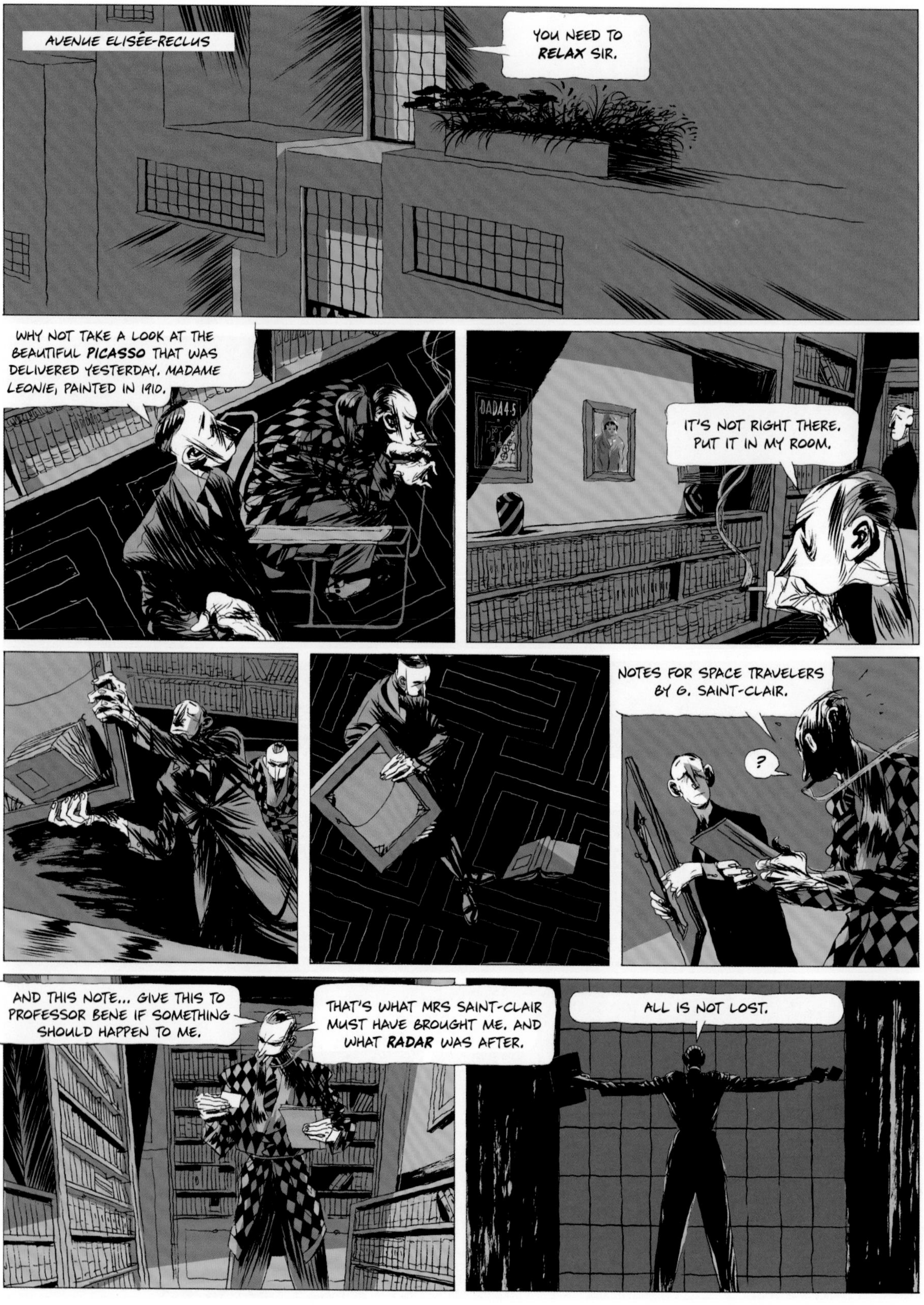
AVENUE ELISÉE-RECLUS
YOU NEED TO RELAX SIR.
WHY NOT TAKE A LOOK AT THE BEAUTIFUL PICASSO THAT WAS DELIVERED YESTERDAY. MADAME LEONIE, PAINTED IN 1910.
DADA 4-5
IT'S NOT RIGHT THERE. PUT IT IN MY ROOM.
NOTES FOR SPACE TRAVELERS BY G. SAINT-CLAIR.
?
AND THIS NOTE... GIVE THIS TO PROFESSOR BENE IF SOMETHING SHOULD HAPPEN TO ME.
THAT'S WHAT MRS SAINT-CLAIR MUST HAVE BROUGHT ME. AND WHAT RADAR WAS AFTER.
ALL IS NOT LOST.

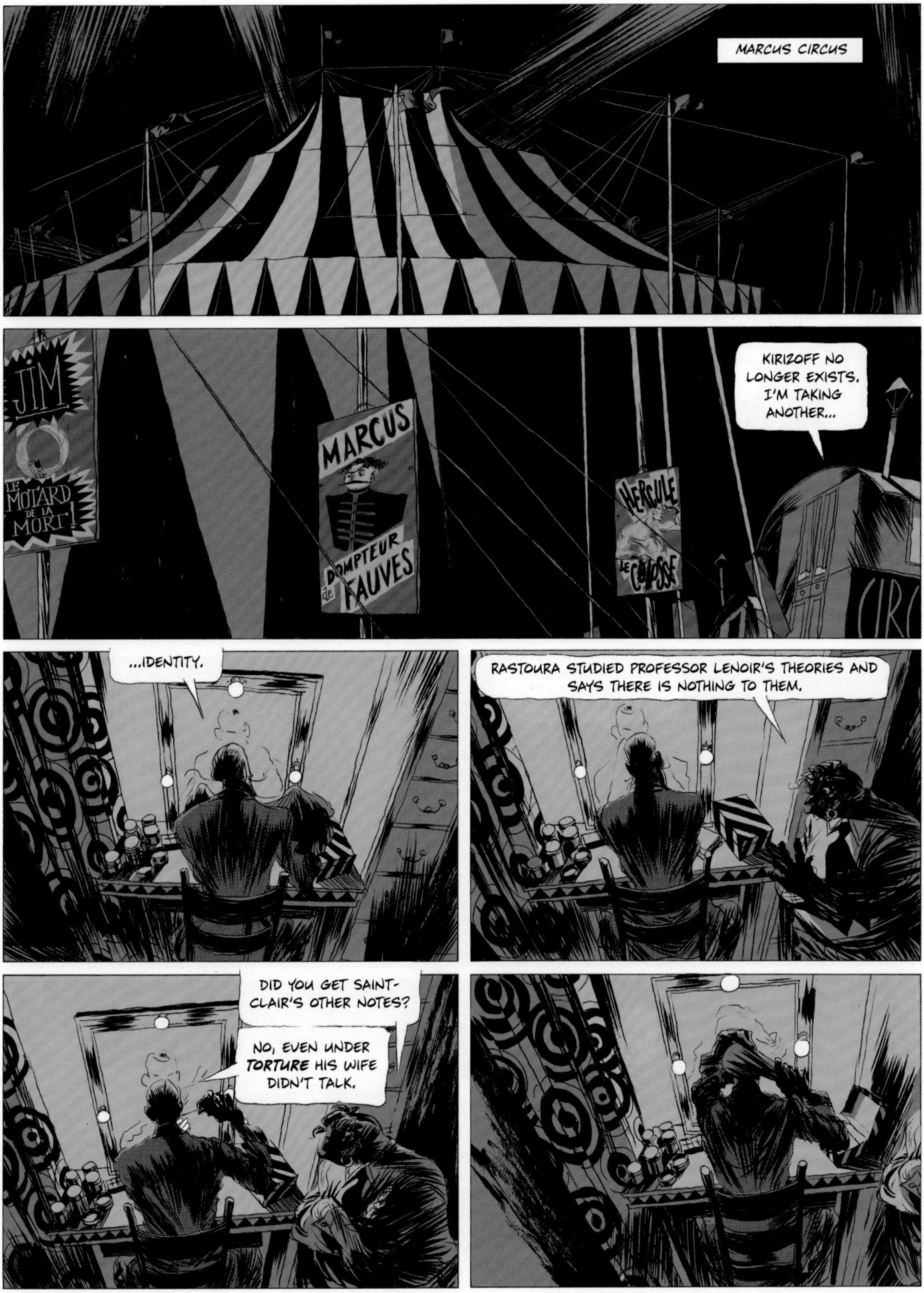
MARCUS CIRCUS
JIM
LE MOTARD DE LA MORT!
MARCUS
DOMPTEUR de FAUVES
HERCULE
KIRIZOFF NO LONGER EXISTS. I'M TAKING ANOTHER...
...IDENTITY.
RASTOURA STUDIED PROFESSOR LENOIR'S THEORIES AND SAYS THERE IS NOTHING TO THEM.
DID YOU GET SAINT-CLAIR'S OTHER NOTES?
NO, EVEN UNDER **TORTURE** HIS WIFE DIDN'T TALK.

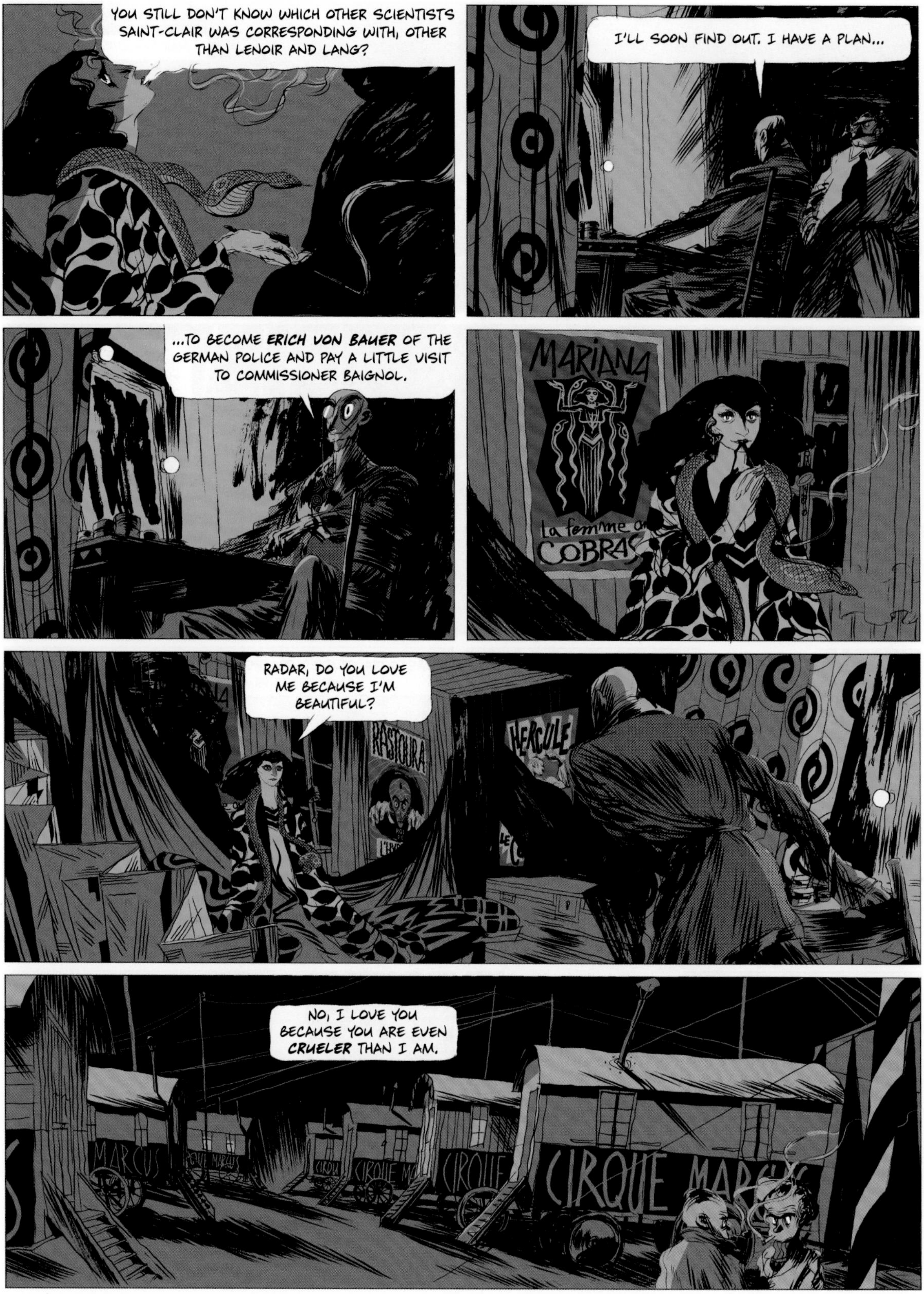
YOU STILL DON'T KNOW WHICH OTHER SCIENTISTS SAINT-CLAIR WAS CORRESPONDING WITH, OTHER THAN LENOIR AND LANG?
I'LL SOON FIND OUT. I HAVE A PLAN...
...TO BECOME **ERICH VON BAUER** OF THE GERMAN POLICE AND PAY A LITTLE VISIT TO COMMISSIONER BAIGNOL.
MARIANA
La femme aux COBRAS
RADAR, DO YOU LOVE ME BECAUSE I'M BEAUTIFUL?
HERCULE
RASTOURA
NO, I LOVE YOU BECAUSE YOU ARE EVEN **CRUELER** THAN I AM.
CIRQUE MARCUS

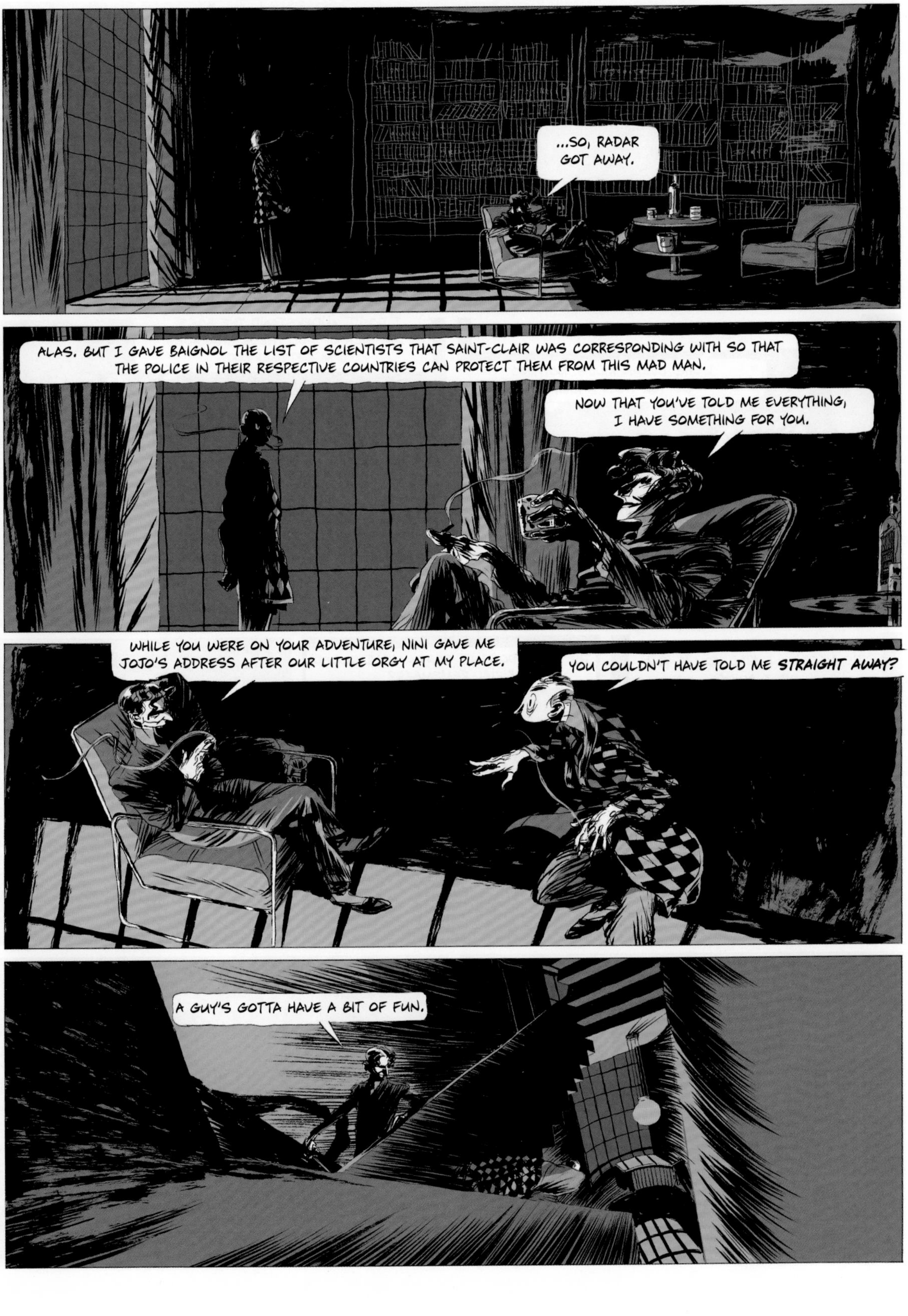
...SO, RADAR GOT AWAY.
ALAS. BUT I GAVE BAIGNOL THE LIST OF SCIENTISTS THAT SAINT-CLAIR WAS CORRESPONDING WITH SO THAT THE POLICE IN THEIR RESPECTIVE COUNTRIES CAN PROTECT THEM FROM THIS MAD MAN.
NOW THAT YOU'VE TOLD ME EVERYTHING, I HAVE SOMETHING FOR YOU.
WHILE YOU WERE ON YOUR ADVENTURE, NINI GAVE ME JOJO'S ADDRESS AFTER OUR LITTLE ORGY AT MY PLACE.
YOU COULDN'T HAVE TOLD ME **STRAIGHT AWAY?**
A GUY'S GOTTA HAVE A BIT OF FUN.

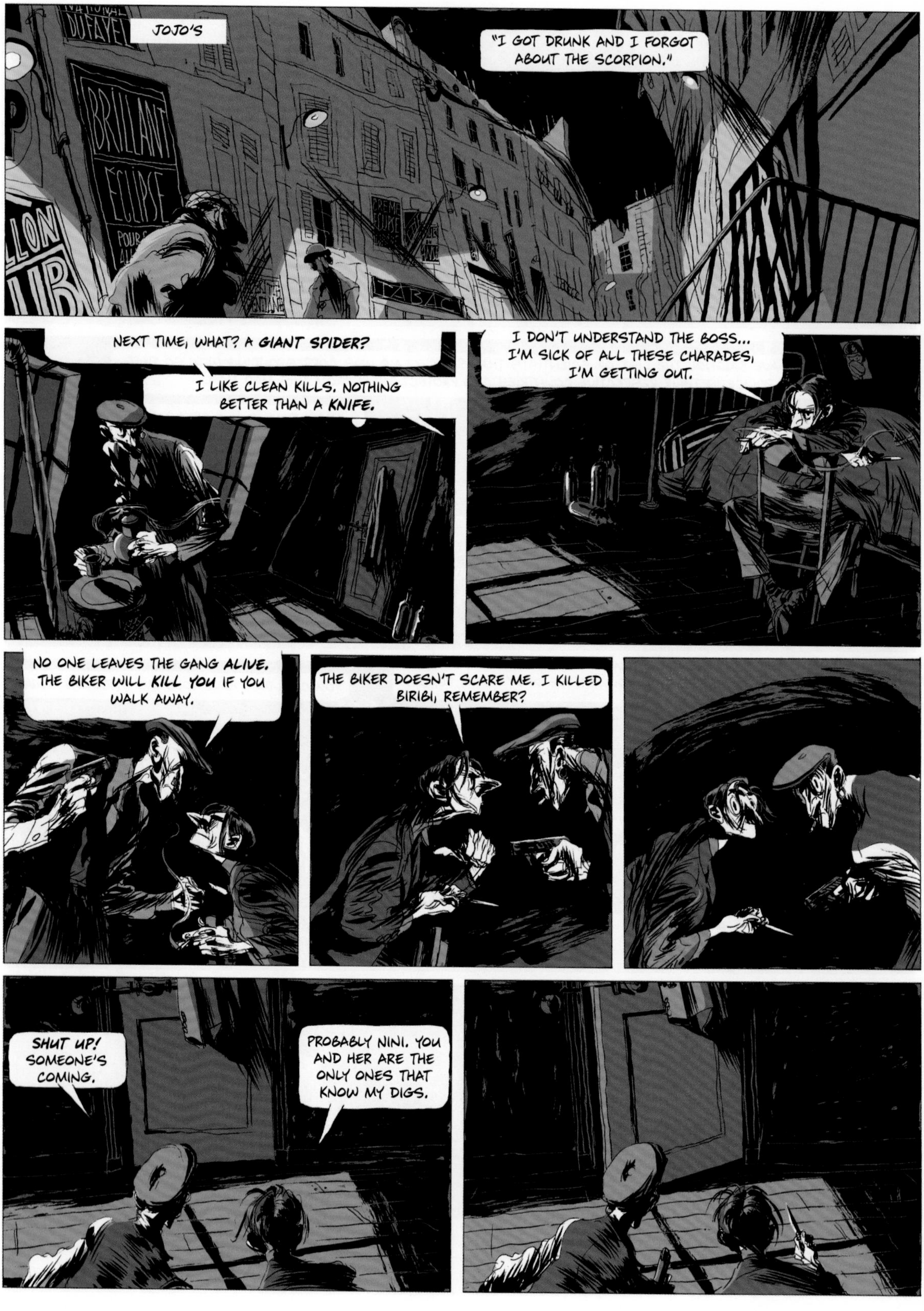
JOJO'S
"I GOT DRUNK AND I FORGOT ABOUT THE SCORPION."
BRILANT ÉCLIPSE
TABAC
NEXT TIME, WHAT? A GIANT SPIDER?
I LIKE CLEAN KILLS. NOTHING BETTER THAN A KNIFE.
I DON'T UNDERSTAND THE BOSS... I'M SICK OF ALL THESE CHARADES, I'M GETTING OUT.
NO ONE LEAVES THE GANG ALIVE. THE BIKER WILL KILL YOU IF YOU WALK AWAY.
THE BIKER DOESN'T SCARE ME. I KILLED BIRIBI, REMEMBER?
SHUT UP! SOMEONE'S COMING.
PROBABLY NINI. YOU AND HER ARE THE ONLY ONES THAT KNOW MY DIGS.

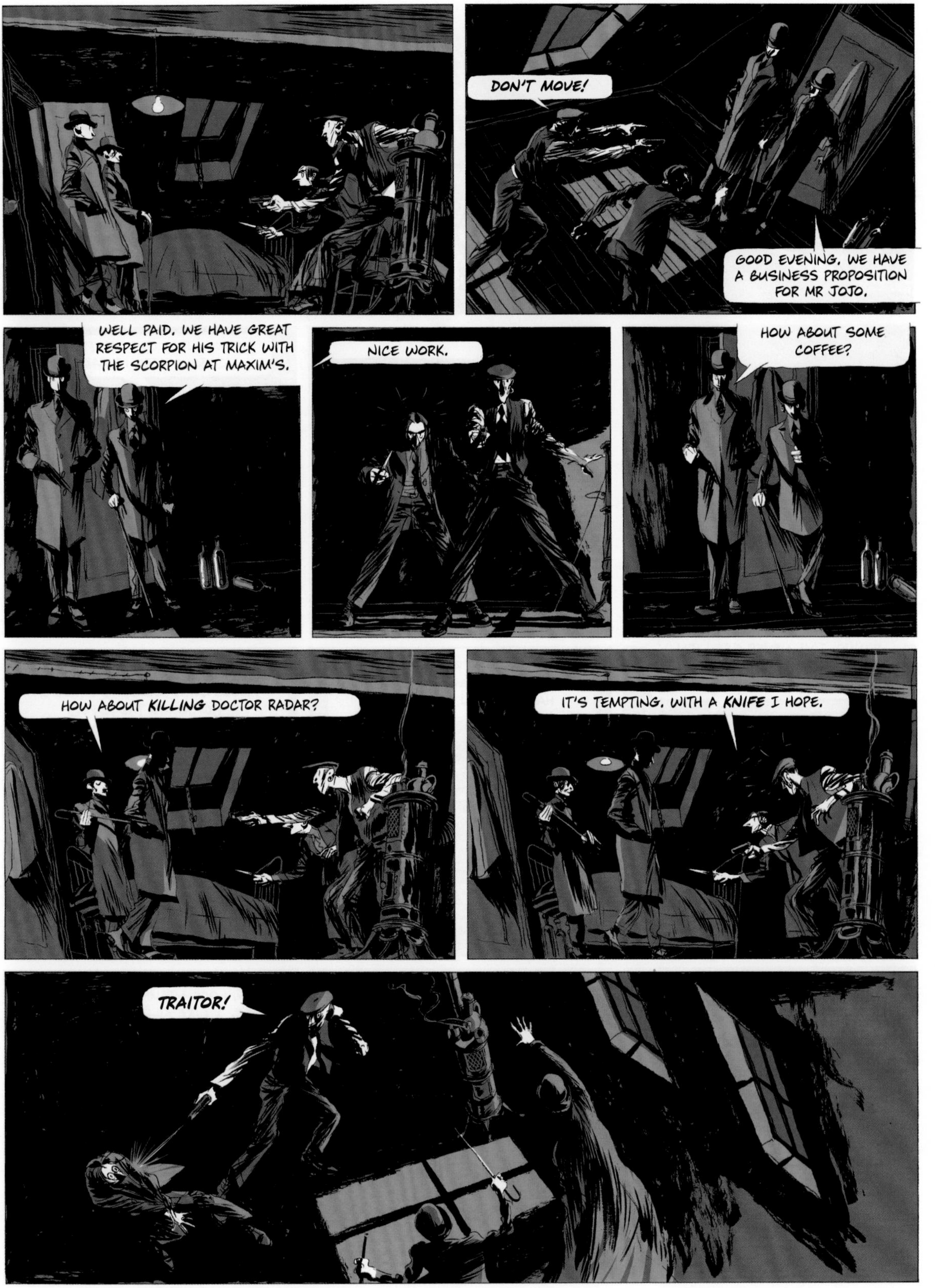
DON'T MOVE!
GOOD EVENING. WE HAVE A BUSINESS PROPOSITION FOR MR JOJO.
WELL PAID. WE HAVE GREAT RESPECT FOR HIS TRICK WITH THE SCORPION AT MAXIM'S.
NICE WORK.
HOW ABOUT SOME COFFEE?
HOW ABOUT KILLING DOCTOR RADAR?
IT'S TEMPTING. WITH A KNIFE I HOPE.
TRAITOR!

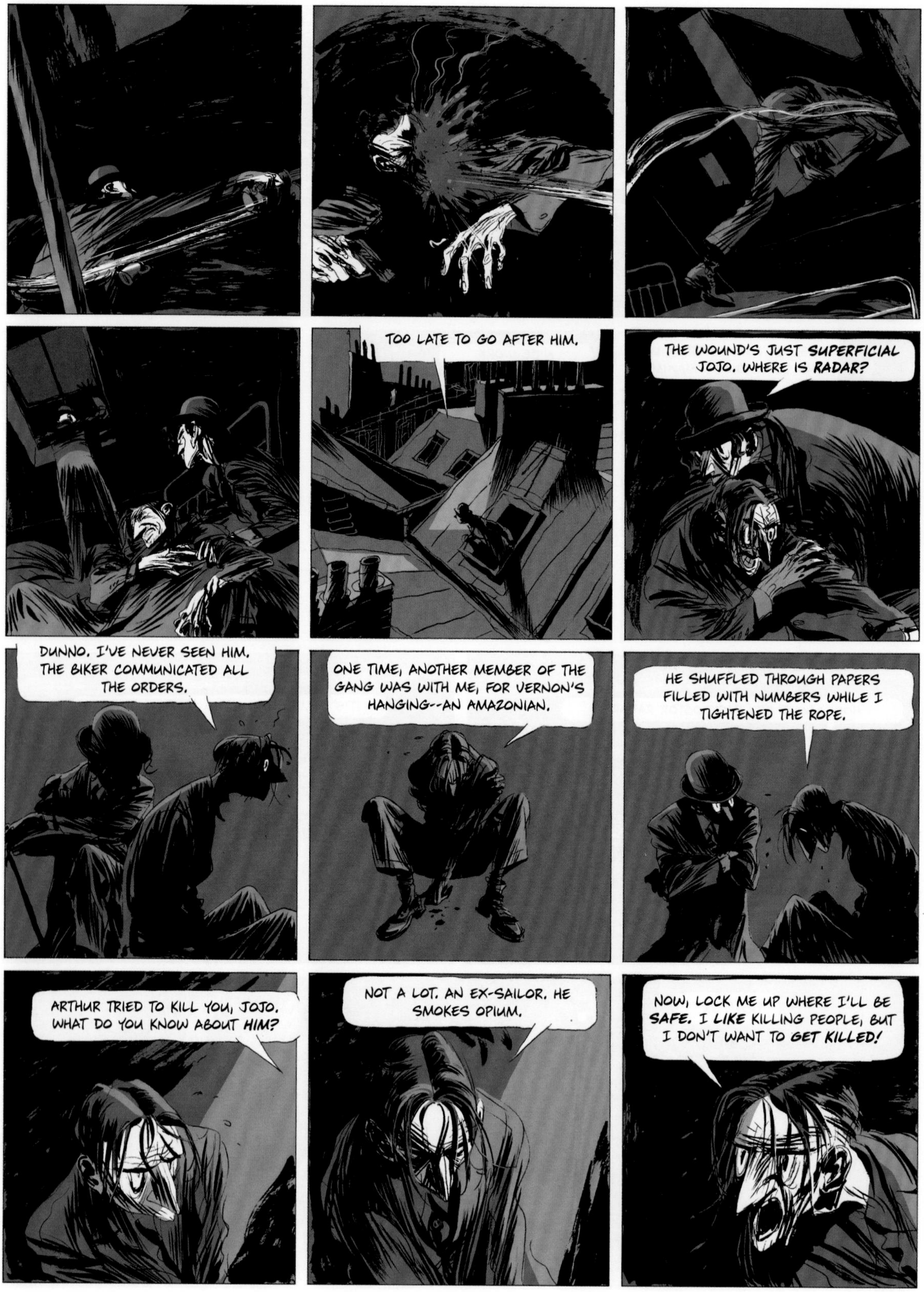
TOO LATE TO GO AFTER HIM.
THE WOUND'S JUST SUPERFICIAL JOJO. WHERE IS RADAR?
DUNNO. I'VE NEVER SEEN HIM. THE BIKER COMMUNICATED ALL THE ORDERS.
ONE TIME, ANOTHER MEMBER OF THE GANG WAS WITH ME, FOR VERNON'S HANGING--AN AMAZONIAN.
HE SHUFFLED THROUGH PAPERS FILLED WITH NUMBERS WHILE I TIGHTENED THE ROPE.
ARTHUR TRIED TO KILL YOU, JOJO. WHAT DO YOU KNOW ABOUT HIM?
NOT A LOT. AN EX-SAILOR. HE SMOKES OPIUM.
NOW, LOCK ME UP WHERE I'LL BE SAFE. I LIKE KILLING PEOPLE, BUT I DON'T WANT TO GET KILLED!

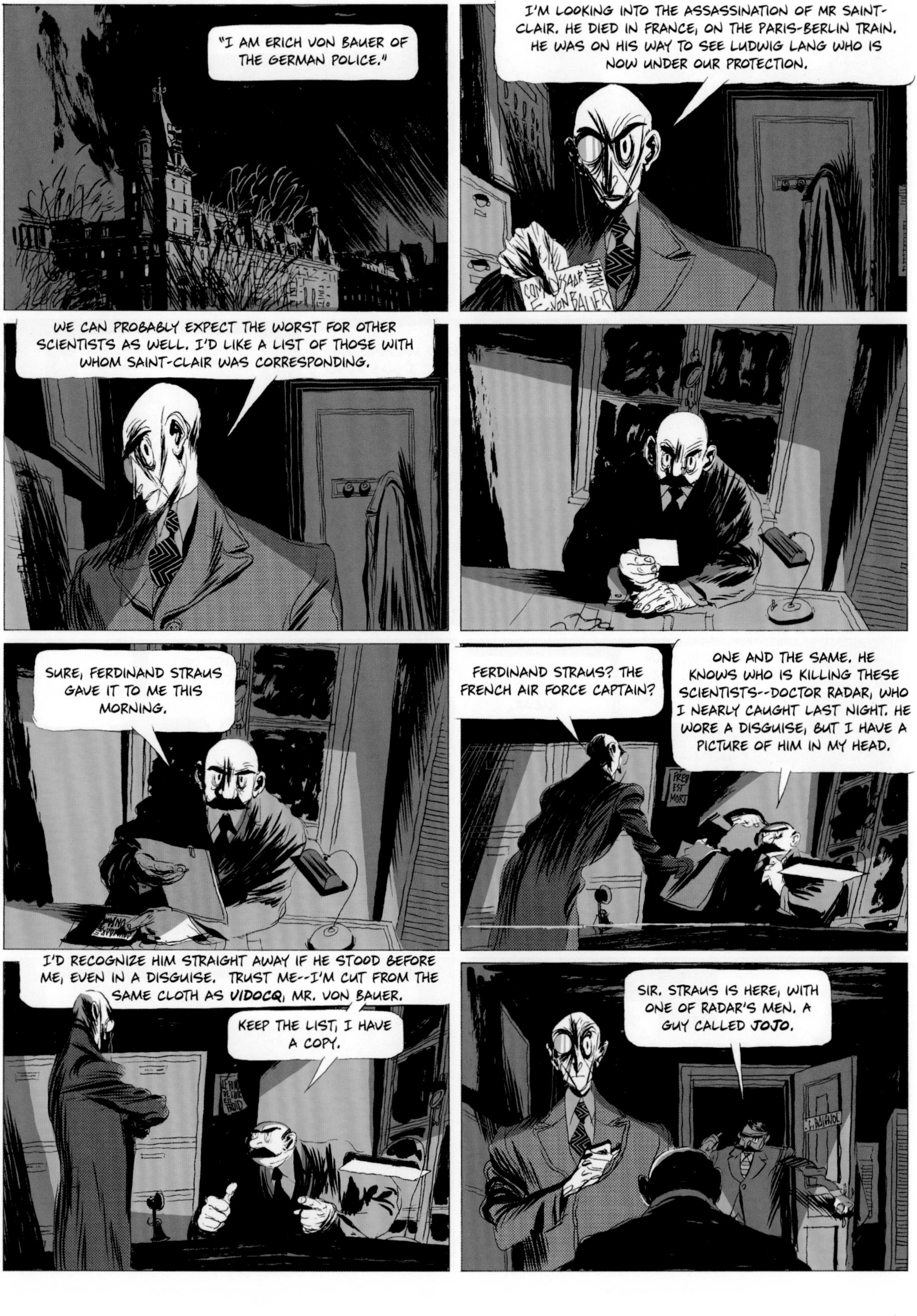
"I AM ERICH VON BAUER OF THE GERMAN POLICE."
I'M LOOKING INTO THE ASSASSINATION OF MR SAINT-CLAIR. HE DIED IN FRANCE, ON THE PARIS-BERLIN TRAIN. HE WAS ON HIS WAY TO SEE LUDWIG LANG WHO IS NOW UNDER OUR PROTECTION.
WE CAN PROBABLY EXPECT THE WORST FOR OTHER SCIENTISTS AS WELL. I'D LIKE A LIST OF THOSE WITH WHOM SAINT-CLAIR WAS CORRESPONDING.
SURE, FERDINAND STRAUS GAVE IT TO ME THIS MORNING.
FERDINAND STRAUS? THE FRENCH AIR FORCE CAPTAIN?
ONE AND THE SAME. HE KNOWS WHO IS KILLING THESE SCIENTISTS--DOCTOR RADAR, WHO I NEARLY CAUGHT LAST NIGHT. HE WORE A DISGUISE, BUT I HAVE A PICTURE OF HIM IN MY HEAD.
I'D RECOGNIZE HIM STRAIGHT AWAY IF HE STOOD BEFORE ME, EVEN IN A DISGUISE. TRUST ME--I'M CUT FROM THE SAME CLOTH AS VIDOCQ, MR. VON BAUER.
KEEP THE LIST, I HAVE A COPY.
SIR. STRAUS IS HERE, WITH ONE OF RADAR'S MEN. A GUY CALLED JOJO.

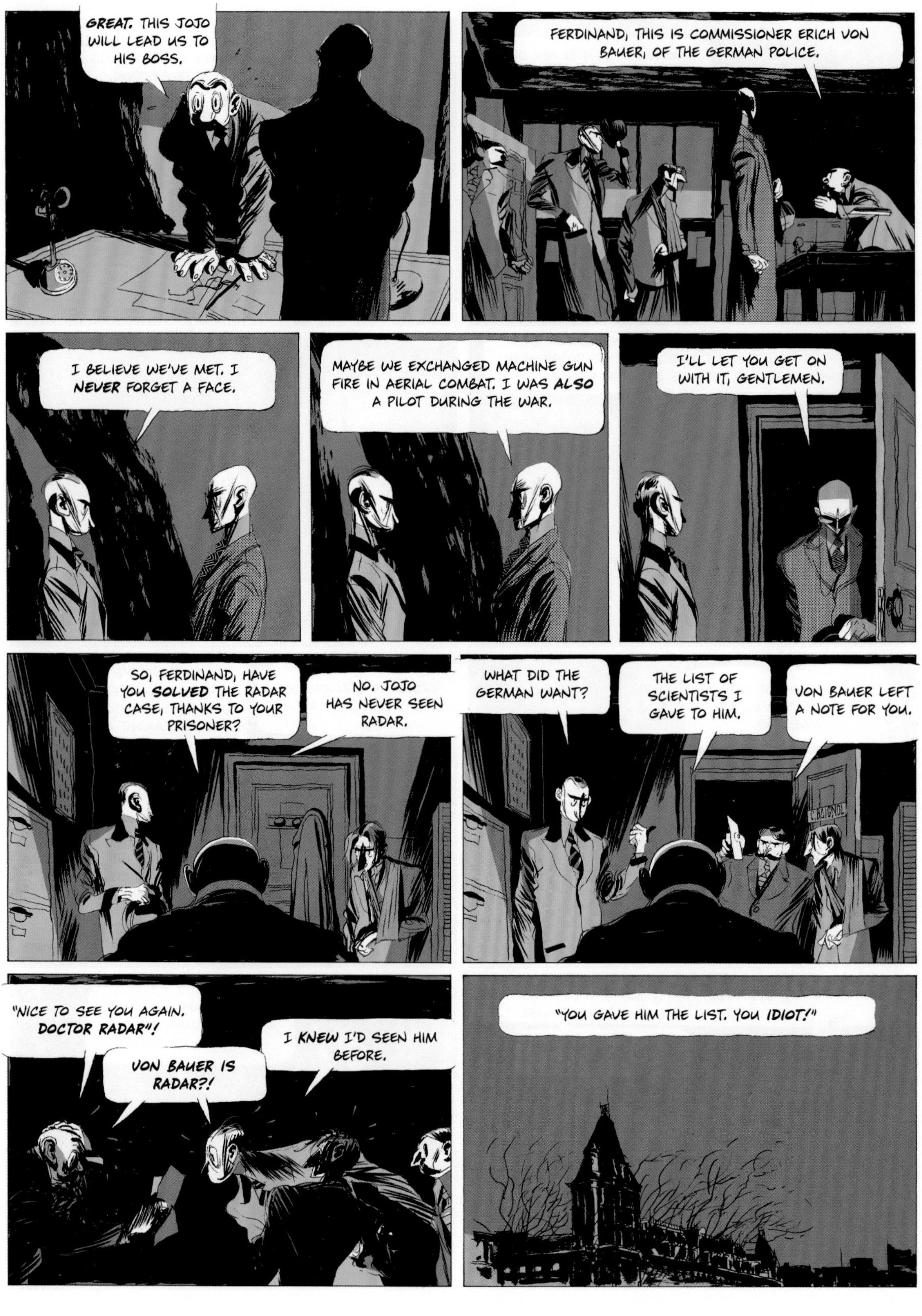
GREAT. THIS JOJO WILL LEAD US TO HIS BOSS.
FERDINAND, THIS IS COMMISSIONER ERICH VON BAUER, OF THE GERMAN POLICE.
I BELIEVE WE'VE MET. I NEVER FORGET A FACE.
MAYBE WE EXCHANGED MACHINE GUN FIRE IN AERIAL COMBAT. I WAS ALSO A PILOT DURING THE WAR.
I'LL LET YOU GET ON WITH IT, GENTLEMEN.
SO, FERDINAND, HAVE YOU SOLVED THE RADAR CASE, THANKS TO YOUR PRISONER?
NO. JOJO HAS NEVER SEEN RADAR.
WHAT DID THE GERMAN WANT?
THE LIST OF SCIENTISTS I GAVE TO HIM.
VON BAUER LEFT A NOTE FOR YOU.
"NICE TO SEE YOU AGAIN. DOCTOR RADAR"!
VON BAUER IS RADAR?!
I KNEW I'D SEEN HIM BEFORE.
"YOU GAVE HIM THE LIST. YOU IDIOT!"

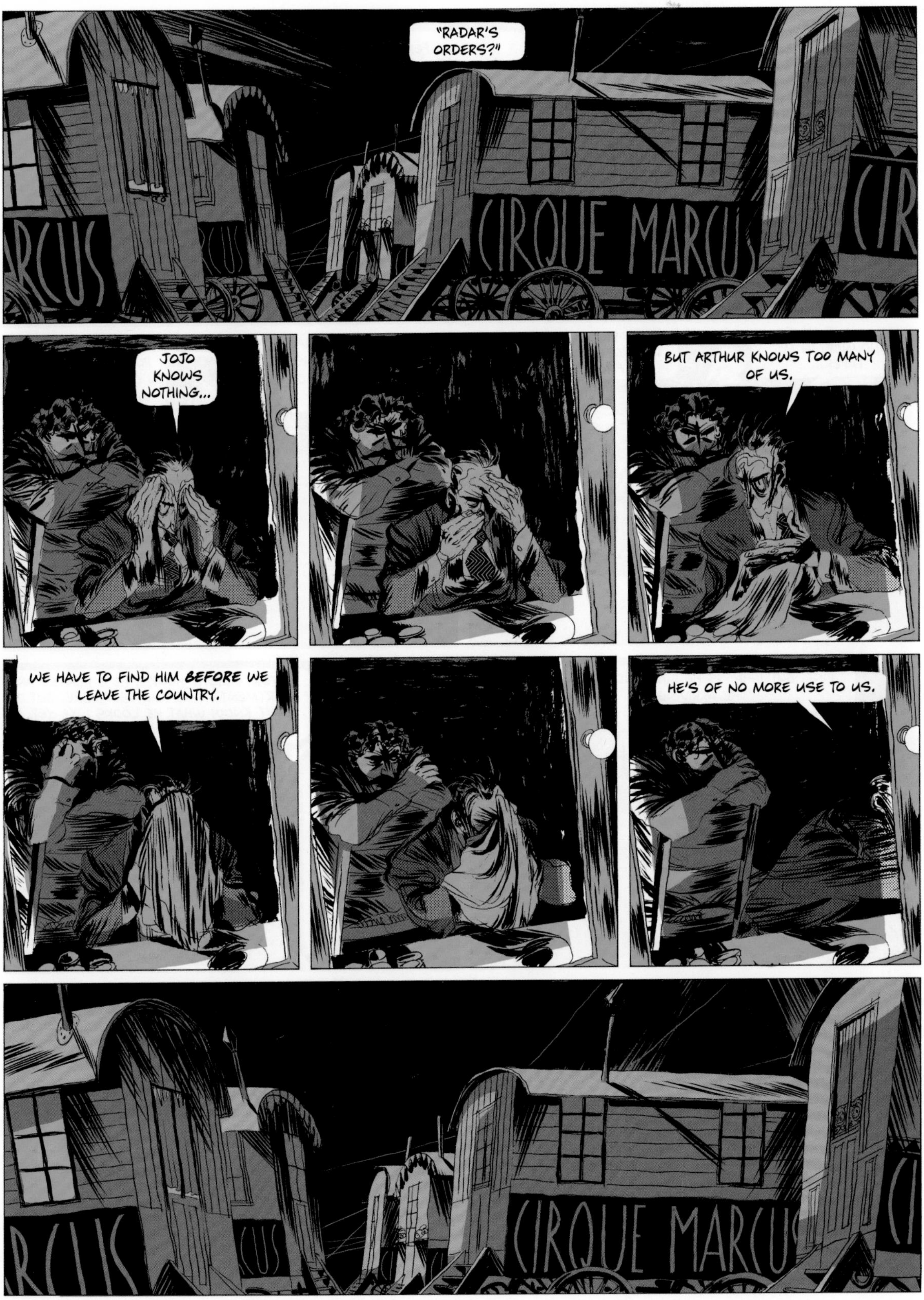
"RADAR'S ORDERS?"
JOJO KNOWS NOTHING...
BUT ARTHUR KNOWS TOO MANY OF US.
WE HAVE TO FIND HIM ***BEFORE*** WE LEAVE THE COUNTRY.
HE'S OF NO MORE USE TO US.
CIRQUE MARCUS

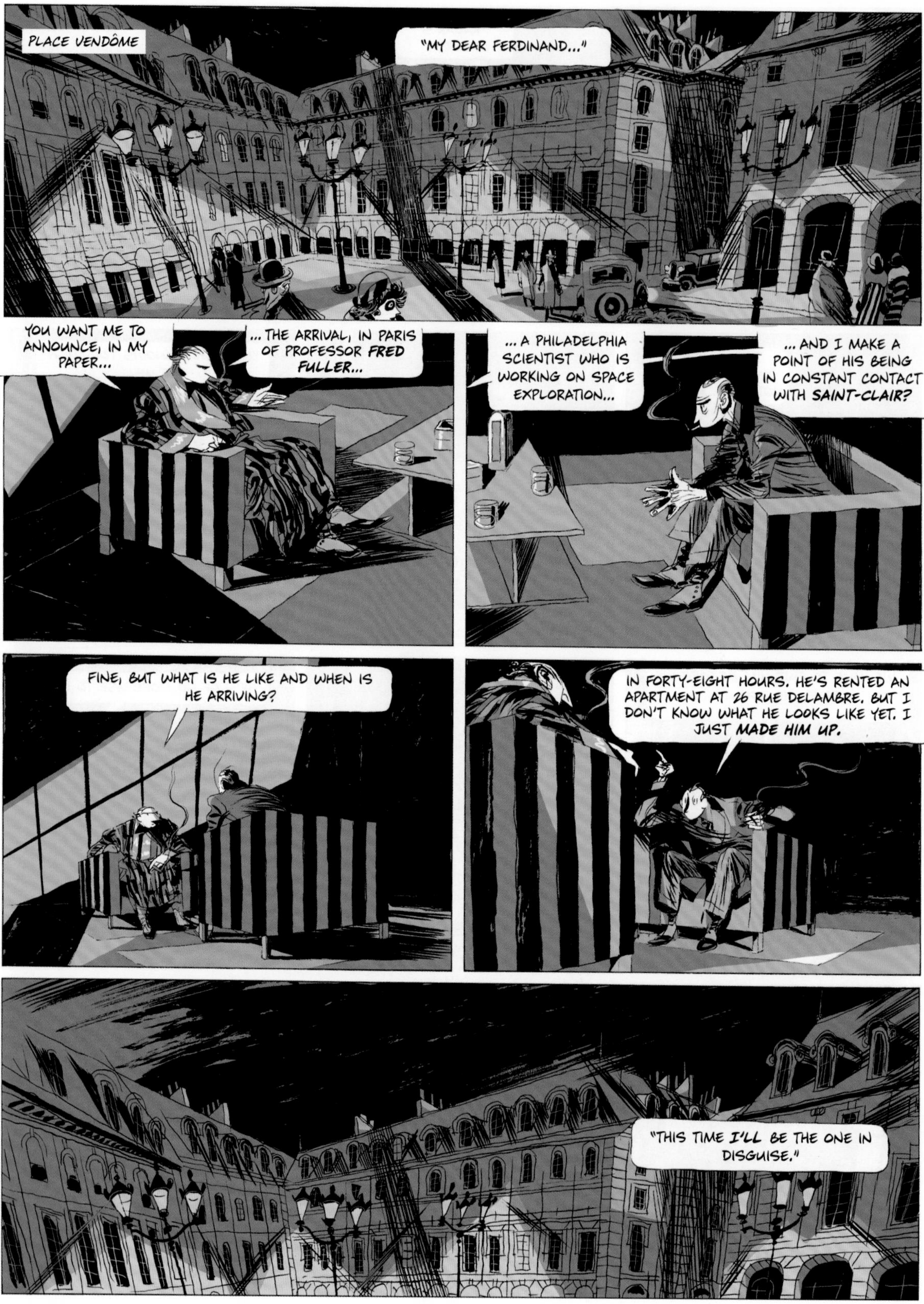
PLACE VENDÔME
"MY DEAR FERDINAND..."
YOU WANT ME TO ANNOUNCE, IN MY PAPER...
... THE ARRIVAL, IN PARIS OF PROFESSOR FRED FULLER...
... A PHILADELPHIA SCIENTIST WHO IS WORKING ON SPACE EXPLORATION...
... AND I MAKE A POINT OF HIS BEING IN CONSTANT CONTACT WITH SAINT-CLAIR?
FINE, BUT WHAT IS HE LIKE AND WHEN IS HE ARRIVING?
IN FORTY-EIGHT HOURS. HE'S RENTED AN APARTMENT AT 26 RUE DELAMBRE. BUT I DON'T KNOW WHAT HE LOOKS LIKE YET. I JUST MADE HIM UP.
"THIS TIME I'LL BE THE ONE IN DISGUISE."

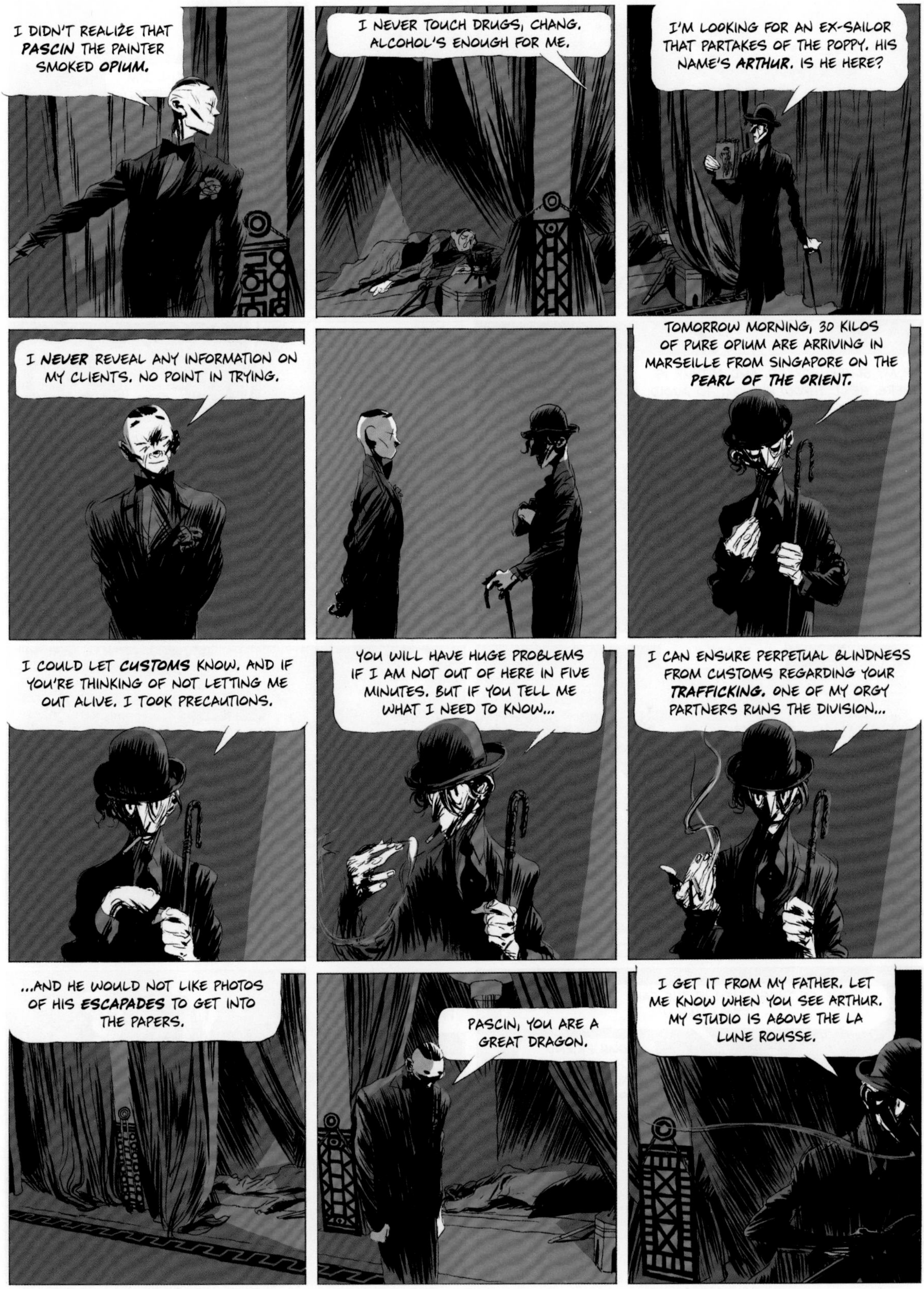
I DIDN'T REALIZE THAT PASCIN THE PAINTER SMOKED OPIUM.
I NEVER TOUCH DRUGS, CHANG. ALCOHOL'S ENOUGH FOR ME.
I'M LOOKING FOR AN EX-SAILOR THAT PARTAKES OF THE POPPY. HIS NAME'S ARTHUR. IS HE HERE?
I NEVER REVEAL ANY INFORMATION ON MY CLIENTS. NO POINT IN TRYING.
TOMORROW MORNING, 30 KILOS OF PURE OPIUM ARE ARRIVING IN MARSEILLE FROM SINGAPORE ON THE PEARL OF THE ORIENT.
I COULD LET CUSTOMS KNOW. AND IF YOU'RE THINKING OF NOT LETTING ME OUT ALIVE, I TOOK PRECAUTIONS.
YOU WILL HAVE HUGE PROBLEMS IF I AM NOT OUT OF HERE IN FIVE MINUTES. BUT IF YOU TELL ME WHAT I NEED TO KNOW...
I CAN ENSURE PERPETUAL BLINDNESS FROM CUSTOMS REGARDING YOUR TRAFFICKING. ONE OF MY ORGY PARTNERS RUNS THE DIVISION...
...AND HE WOULD NOT LIKE PHOTOS OF HIS ESCAPADES TO GET INTO THE PAPERS.
PASCIN, YOU ARE A GREAT DRAGON.
I GET IT FROM MY FATHER. LET ME KNOW WHEN YOU SEE ARTHUR. MY STUDIO IS ABOVE THE LA LUNE ROUSSE.

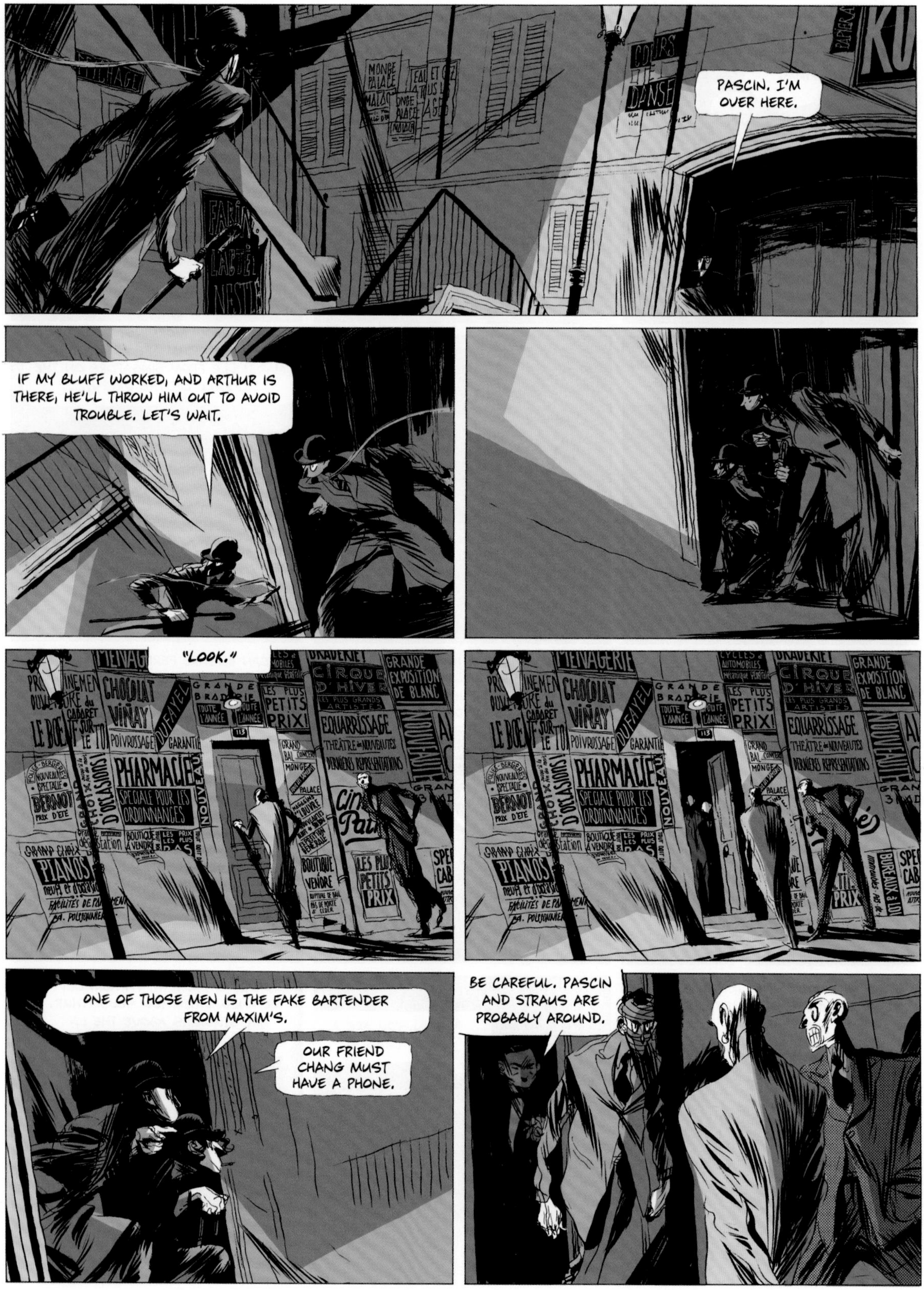
PASCIN. I'M OVER HERE.
IF MY BLUFF WORKED, AND ARTHUR IS THERE, HE'LL THROW HIM OUT TO AVOID TROUBLE. LET'S WAIT.
"LOOK."
ONE OF THOSE MEN IS THE FAKE BARTENDER FROM MAXIM'S.
OUR FRIEND CHANG MUST HAVE A PHONE.
BE CAREFUL. PASCIN AND STRAUS ARE PROBABLY AROUND.

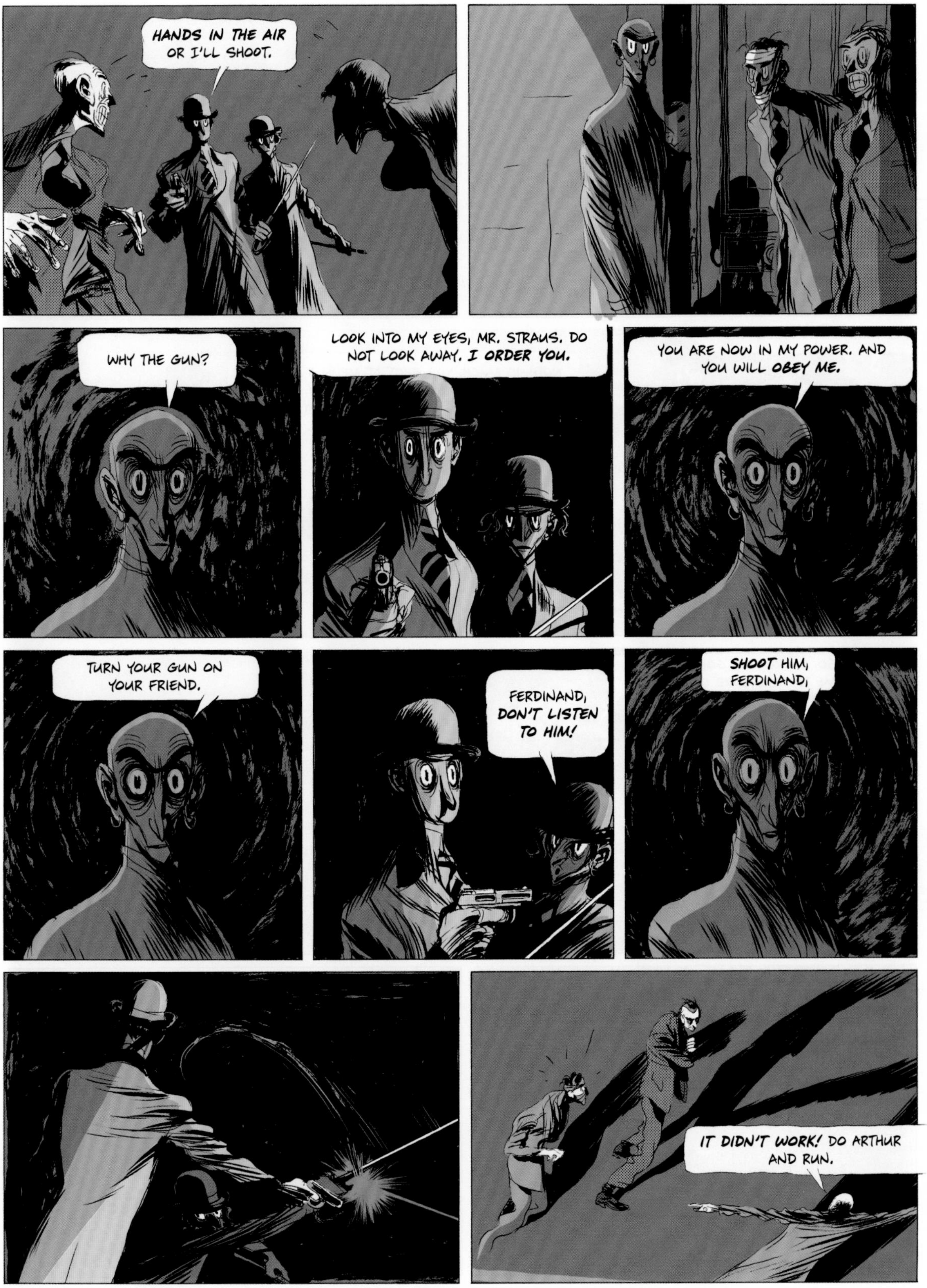
HANDS IN THE AIR OR I'LL SHOOT.
WHY THE GUN?
LOOK INTO MY EYES, MR. STRAUS. DO NOT LOOK AWAY. I ORDER YOU.
YOU ARE NOW IN MY POWER. AND YOU WILL OBEY ME.
TURN YOUR GUN ON YOUR FRIEND.
FERDINAND, DON'T LISTEN TO HIM!
SHOOT HIM, FERDINAND,
IT DIDN'T WORK! DO ARTHUR AND RUN.

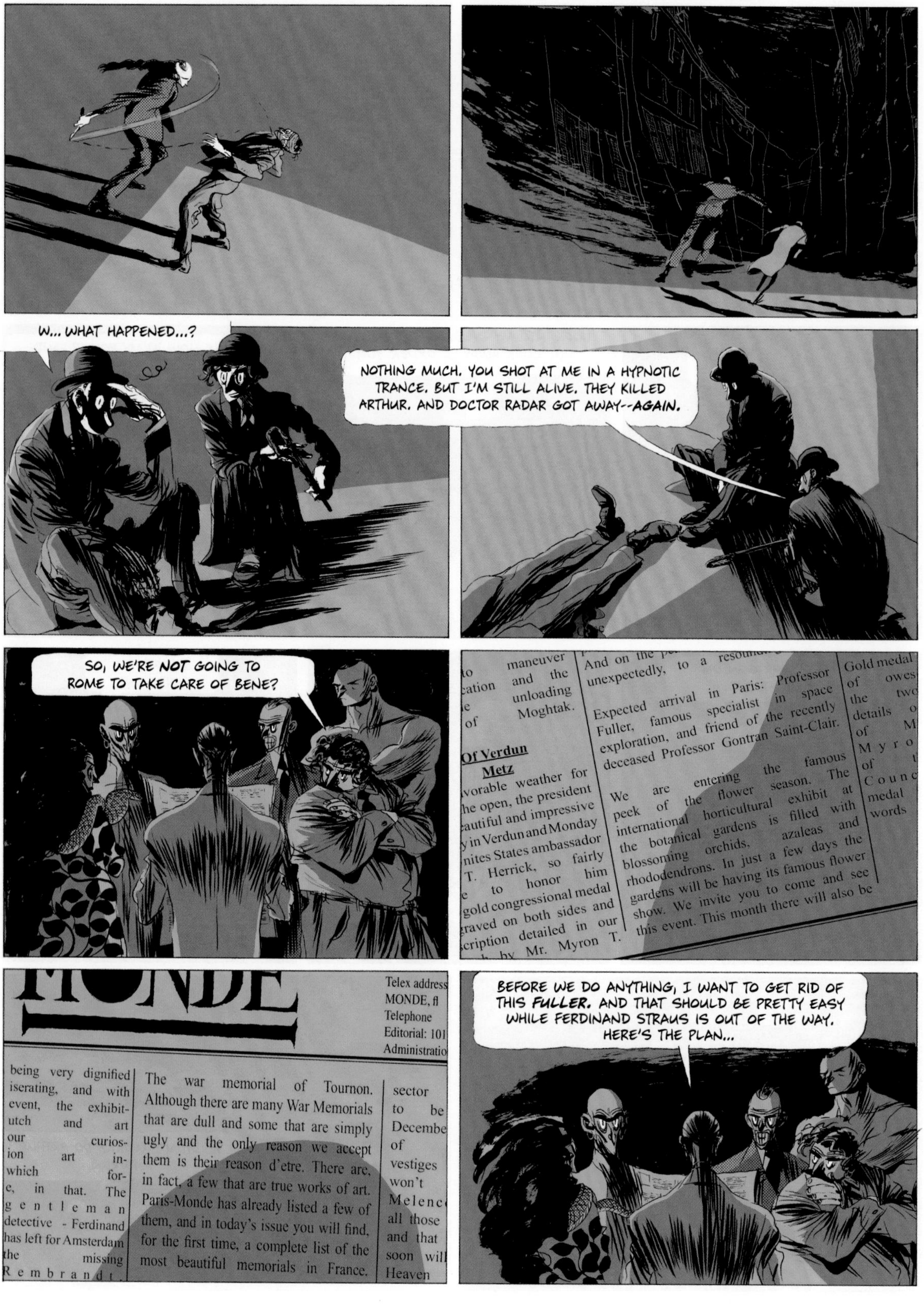
W... WHAT HAPPENED...?
NOTHING MUCH. YOU SHOT AT ME IN A HYPNOTIC TRANCE. BUT I'M STILL ALIVE. THEY KILLED ARTHUR. AND DOCTOR RADAR GOT AWAY--**AGAIN.**
SO, WE'RE **NOT** GOING TO ROME TO TAKE CARE OF BENE?
to maneuver
cation and the
e unloading
of Moghtak.
Of Verdun
Metz
vorable weather for
he open, the president
eautiful and impressive
y in Verdun and Monday
nites States ambassador
T. Herrick, so fairly
e to honor him
gold congressional medal
graved on both sides and
cription detailed in our
h by Mr. Myron T.
And on the
unexpectedly, to a resounding
Expected arrival in Paris: Professor Fuller, famous specialist in space exploration, and friend of the recently deceased Professor Gontran Saint-Clair.
We are entering the famous peek of the flower season. The international horticultural exhibit at the botanical gardens is filled with blossoming orchids, azaleas and rhododendrons. In just a few days the gardens will be having its famous flower show. We invite you to come and see this event. This month there will also be
Gold medal
of owes
the two
details of
of M
Myro
of t
Counc
medal
words
MONDE
Telex address
MONDE, fl
Telephone
Editorial: 101
Administratio
being very dignified
iserating, and with
event, the exhibit-
utch and art
our curios-
ion art in-
which for-
e, in that. The
gentleman
detective - Ferdinand
has left for Amsterdam
the missing
Rembrandt.
The war memorial of Tournon. Although there are many War Memorials that are dull and some that are simply ugly and the only reason we accept them is their reason d'etre. There are, in fact, a few that are true works of art. Paris-Monde has already listed a few of them, and in today's issue you will find, for the first time, a complete list of the most beautiful memorials in France.
sector
to be
Decembe
of
vestiges
won't
Melenc
all those
and that
soon wil
Heaven
BEFORE WE DO ANYTHING, I WANT TO GET RID OF THIS ***FULLER.*** AND THAT SHOULD BE PRETTY EASY WHILE FERDINAND STRAUS IS OUT OF THE WAY. HERE'S THE PLAN...

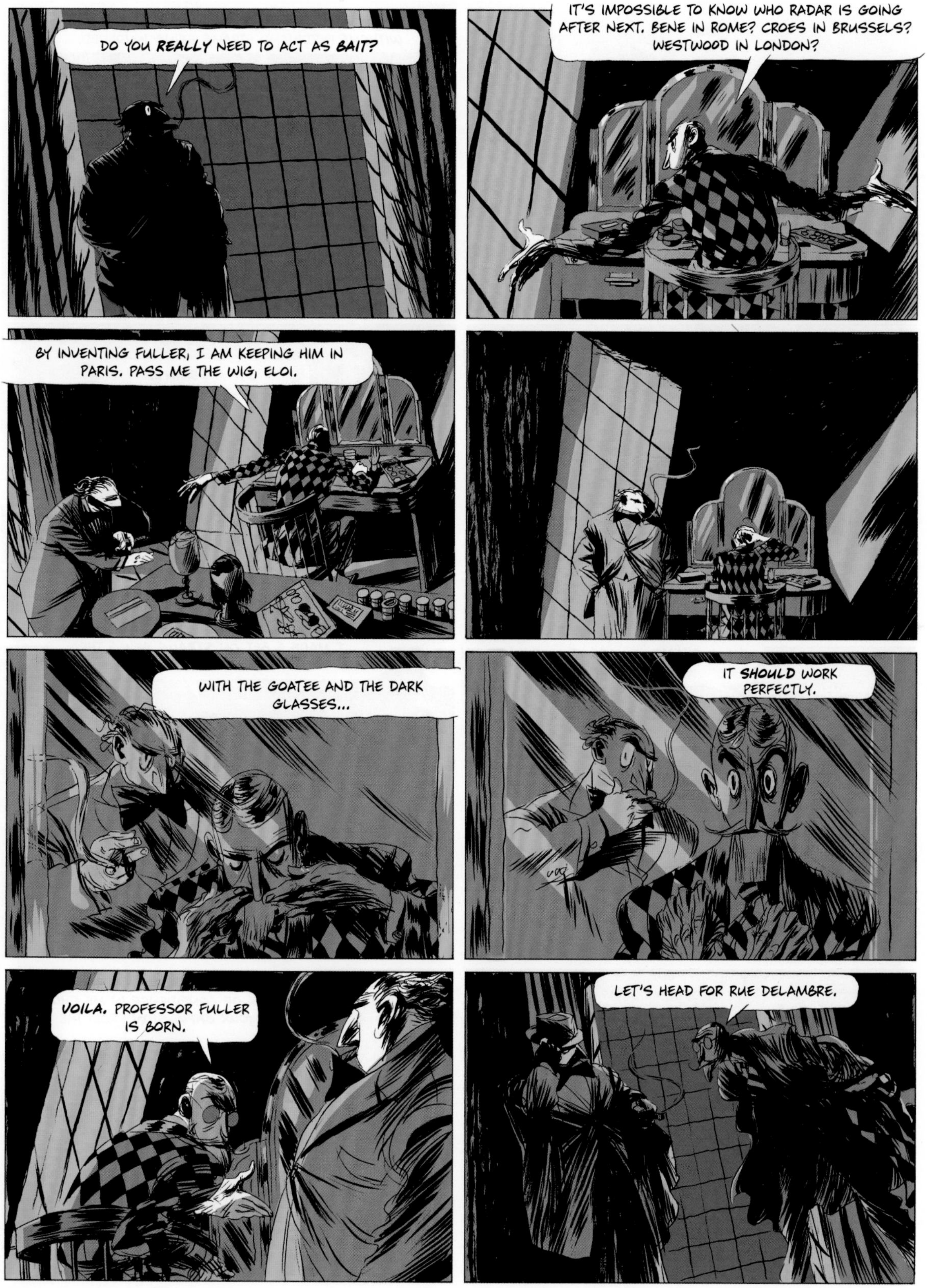
DO YOU **REALLY** NEED TO ACT AS **BAIT?**
IT'S IMPOSSIBLE TO KNOW WHO RADAR IS GOING AFTER NEXT. BENE IN ROME? CROES IN BRUSSELS? WESTWOOD IN LONDON?
BY INVENTING FULLER, I AM KEEPING HIM IN PARIS. PASS ME THE WIG, ELOI.
WITH THE GOATEE AND THE DARK GLASSES...
IT **SHOULD** WORK PERFECTLY.
VOILA. PROFESSOR FULLER IS BORN.
LET'S HEAD FOR RUE DELAMBRE.

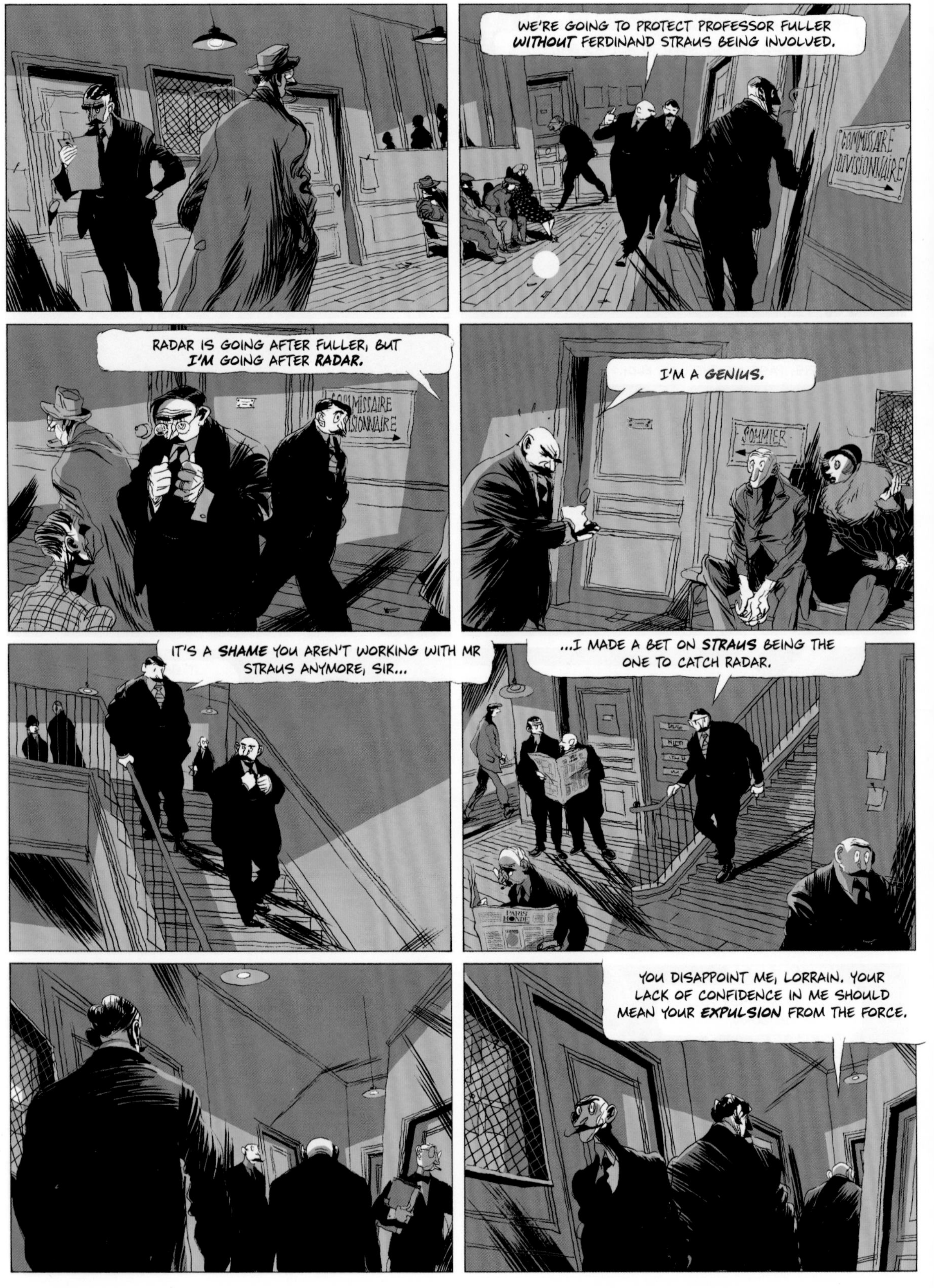
WE'RE GOING TO PROTECT PROFESSOR FULLER *WITHOUT* FERDINAND STRAUS BEING INVOLVED.
COMMISSAIRE DIVISIONNAIRE
RADAR IS GOING AFTER FULLER, BUT *I'M* GOING AFTER *RADAR.*
I'M A *GENIUS.*
SOMMIER
IT'S A *SHAME* YOU AREN'T WORKING WITH MR STRAUS ANYMORE, SIR...
...I MADE A BET ON *STRAUS* BEING THE ONE TO CATCH RADAR.
PARIS MONDE
YOU DISAPPOINT ME, LORRAIN. YOUR LACK OF CONFIDENCE IN ME SHOULD MEAN YOUR *EXPULSION* FROM THE FORCE.

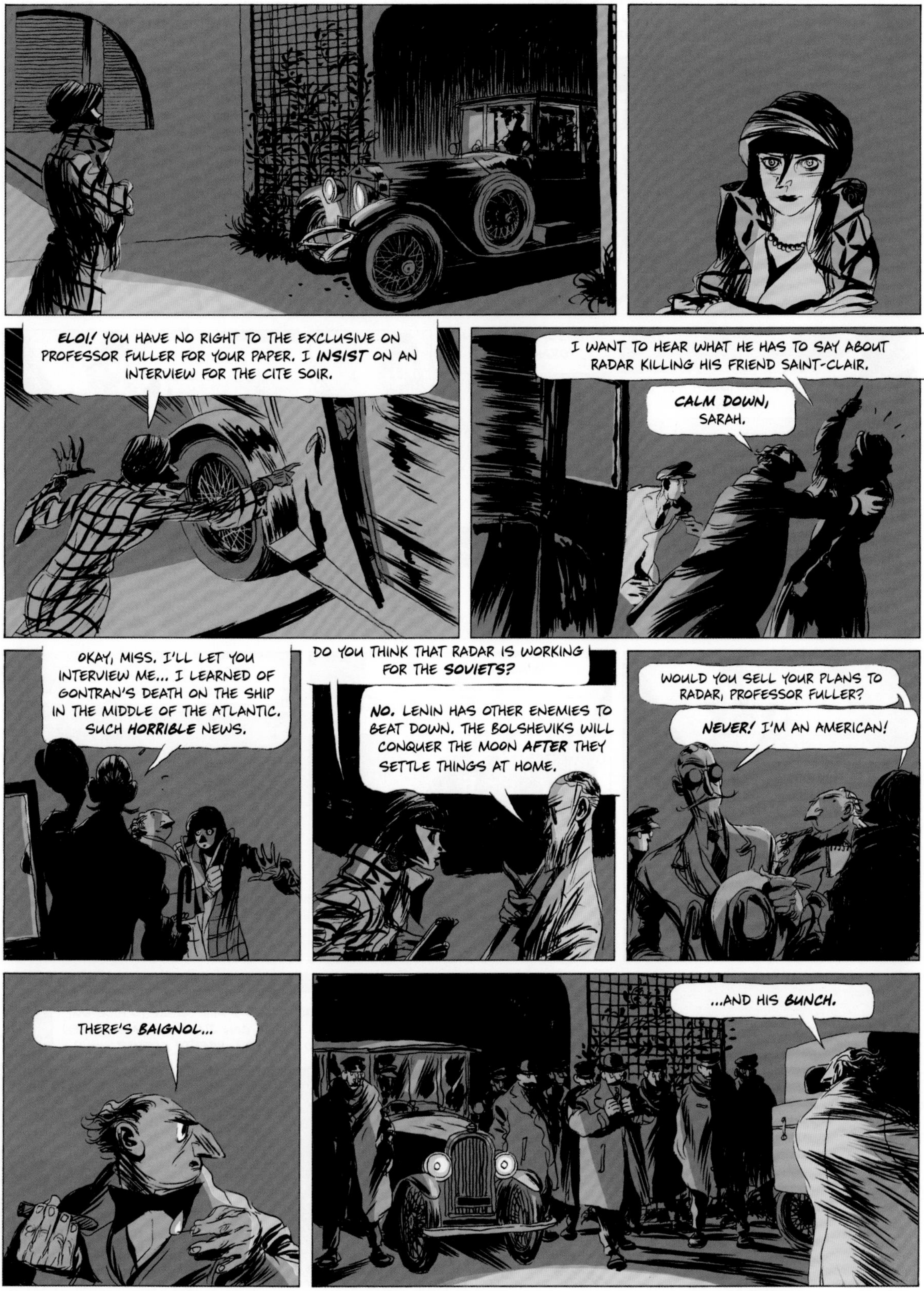
ELOI! YOU HAVE NO RIGHT TO THE EXCLUSIVE ON PROFESSOR FULLER FOR YOUR PAPER. I INSIST ON AN INTERVIEW FOR THE CITE SOIR.
I WANT TO HEAR WHAT HE HAS TO SAY ABOUT RADAR KILLING HIS FRIEND SAINT-CLAIR.
CALM DOWN, SARAH.
OKAY, MISS. I'LL LET YOU INTERVIEW ME... I LEARNED OF GONTRAN'S DEATH ON THE SHIP IN THE MIDDLE OF THE ATLANTIC. SUCH HORRIBLE NEWS.
DO YOU THINK THAT RADAR IS WORKING FOR THE SOVIETS?
NO. LENIN HAS OTHER ENEMIES TO BEAT DOWN. THE BOLSHEVIKS WILL CONQUER THE MOON AFTER THEY SETTLE THINGS AT HOME.
WOULD YOU SELL YOUR PLANS TO RADAR, PROFESSOR FULLER?
NEVER! I'M AN AMERICAN!
THERE'S BAIGNOL...
...AND HIS BUNCH.

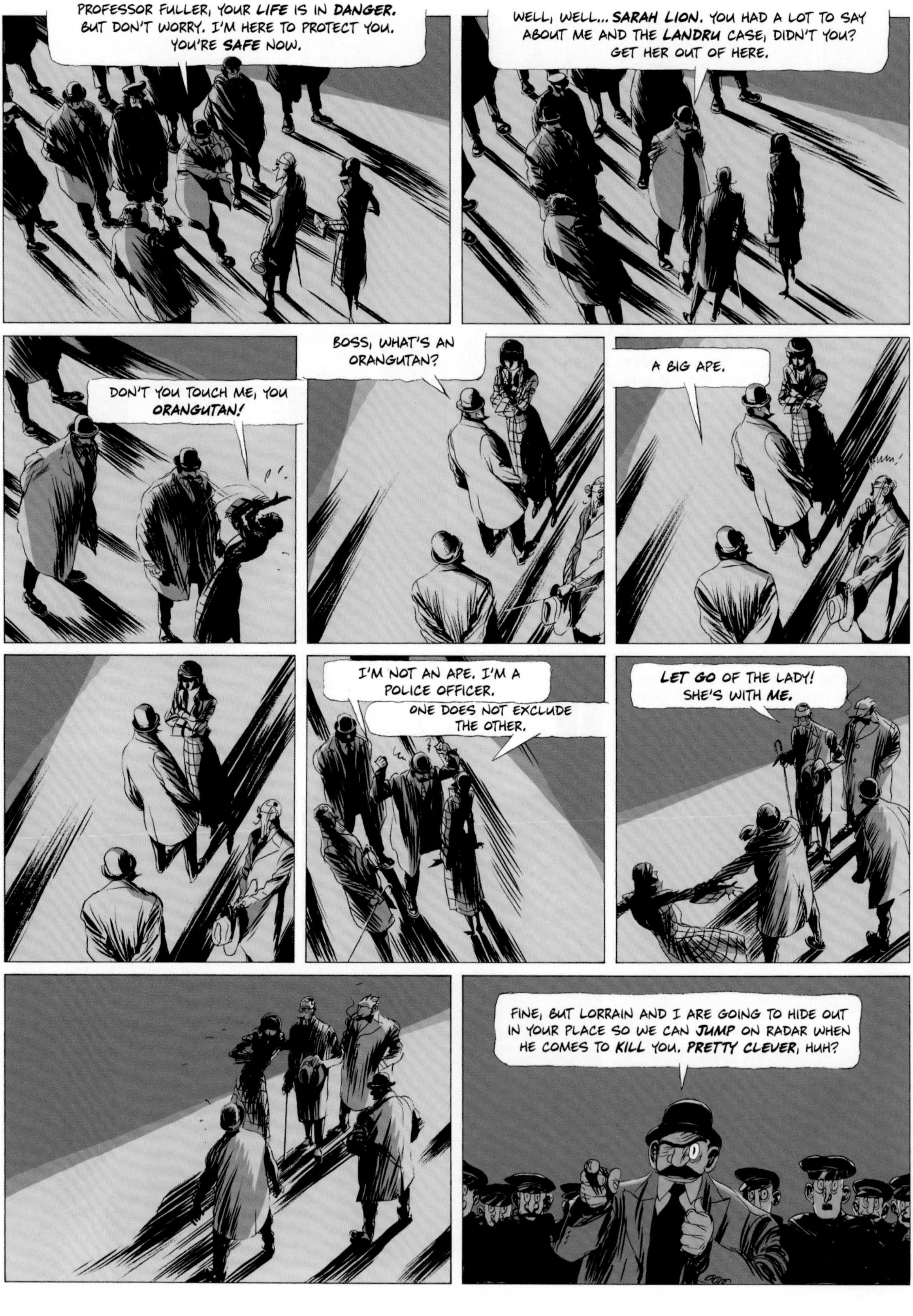
PROFESSOR FULLER, YOUR **LIFE** IS IN **DANGER.** BUT DON'T WORRY. I'M HERE TO PROTECT YOU. YOU'RE **SAFE** NOW.
WELL, WELL... **SARAH LION.** YOU HAD A LOT TO SAY ABOUT ME AND THE **LANDRU** CASE, DIDN'T YOU? GET HER OUT OF HERE.
DON'T YOU TOUCH ME, YOU **ORANGUTAN!**
BOSS, WHAT'S AN ORANGUTAN?
A BIG APE.
HUM!
I'M NOT AN APE. I'M A POLICE OFFICER.
ONE DOES NOT EXCLUDE THE OTHER.
LET GO OF THE LADY! SHE'S WITH **ME.**
FINE, BUT LORRAIN AND I ARE GOING TO HIDE OUT IN YOUR PLACE SO WE CAN **JUMP** ON RADAR WHEN HE COMES TO **KILL** YOU. **PRETTY CLEVER,** HUH?

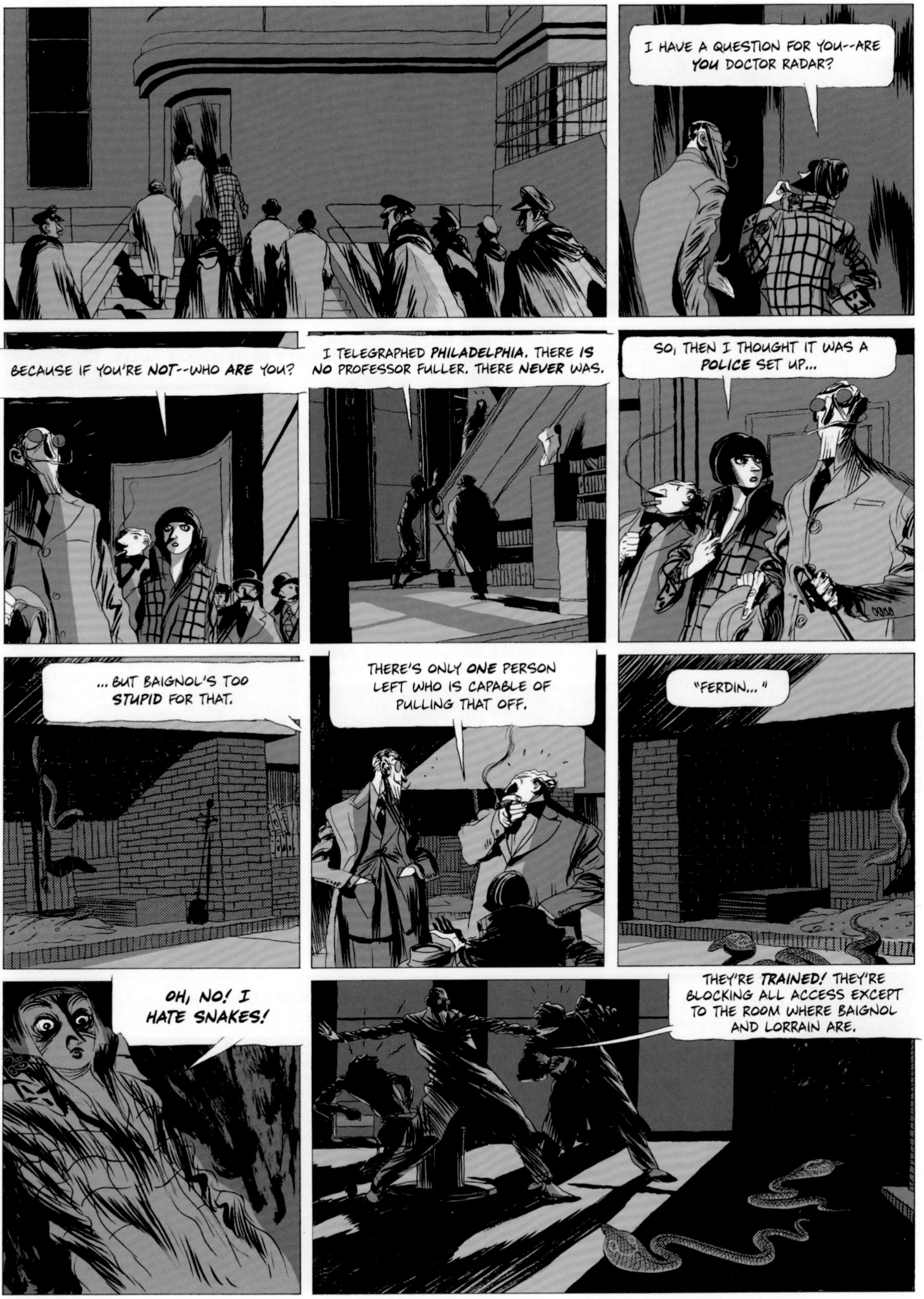
I HAVE A QUESTION FOR YOU--ARE YOU DOCTOR RADAR?
BECAUSE IF YOU'RE NOT--WHO ARE YOU?
I TELEGRAPHED PHILADELPHIA. THERE IS NO PROFESSOR FULLER. THERE NEVER WAS.
SO, THEN I THOUGHT IT WAS A POLICE SET UP...
...BUT BAIGNOL'S TOO STUPID FOR THAT.
THERE'S ONLY ONE PERSON LEFT WHO IS CAPABLE OF PULLING THAT OFF.
"FERDIN..."
OH, NO! I HATE SNAKES!
THEY'RE TRAINED! THEY'RE BLOCKING ALL ACCESS EXCEPT TO THE ROOM WHERE BAIGNOL AND LORRAIN ARE.

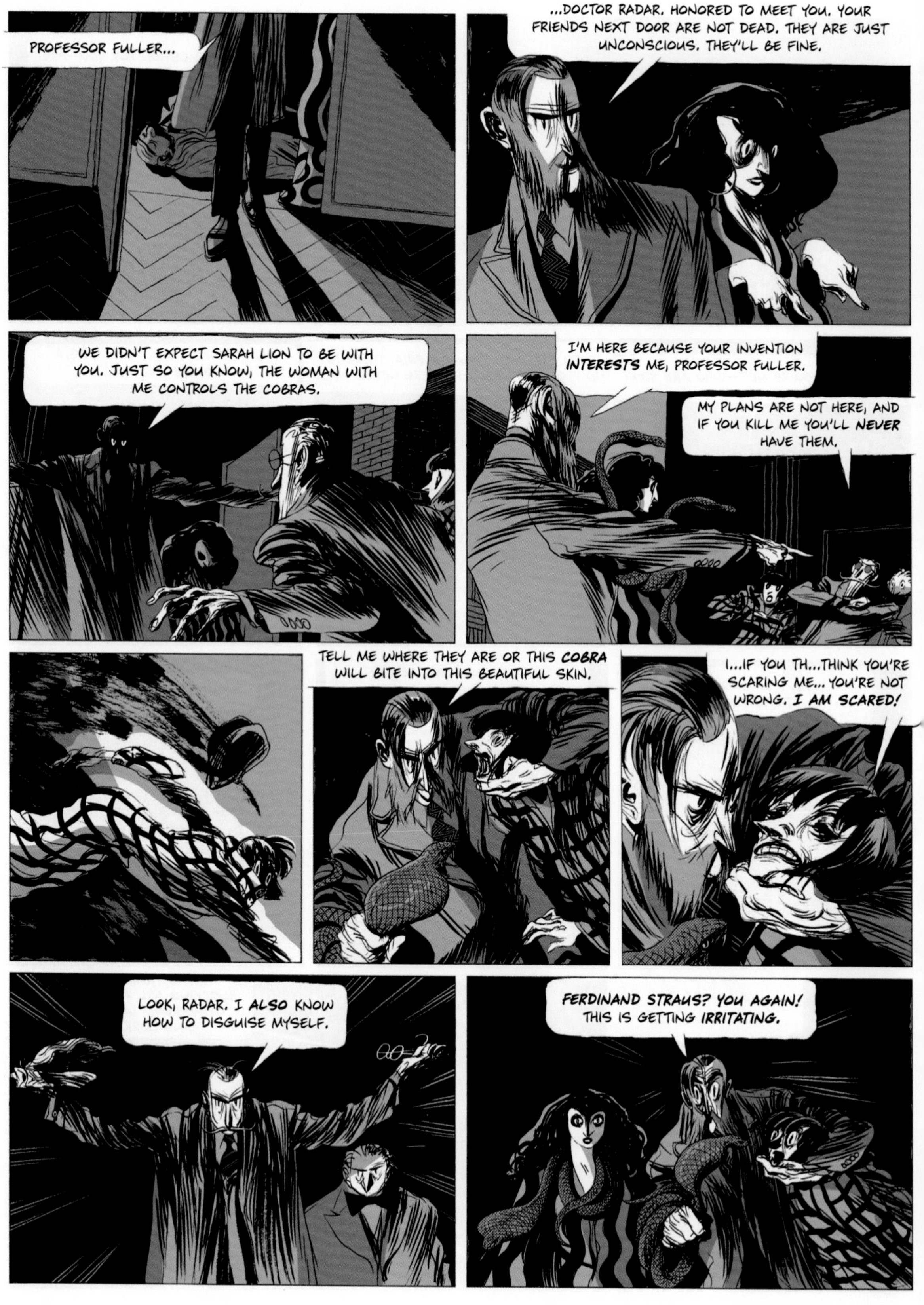
PROFESSOR FULLER...
...DOCTOR RADAR. HONORED TO MEET YOU. YOUR FRIENDS NEXT DOOR ARE NOT DEAD. THEY ARE JUST UNCONSCIOUS. THEY'LL BE FINE.
WE DIDN'T EXPECT SARAH LION TO BE WITH YOU. JUST SO YOU KNOW, THE WOMAN WITH ME CONTROLS THE COBRAS.
I'M HERE BECAUSE YOUR INVENTION INTERESTS ME, PROFESSOR FULLER.
MY PLANS ARE NOT HERE, AND IF YOU KILL ME YOU'LL NEVER HAVE THEM.
TELL ME WHERE THEY ARE OR THIS COBRA WILL BITE INTO THIS BEAUTIFUL SKIN.
I...IF YOU TH...THINK YOU'RE SCARING ME... YOU'RE NOT WRONG. I AM SCARED!
LOOK, RADAR. I ALSO KNOW HOW TO DISGUISE MYSELF.
FERDINAND STRAUS? YOU AGAIN! THIS IS GETTING IRRITATING.

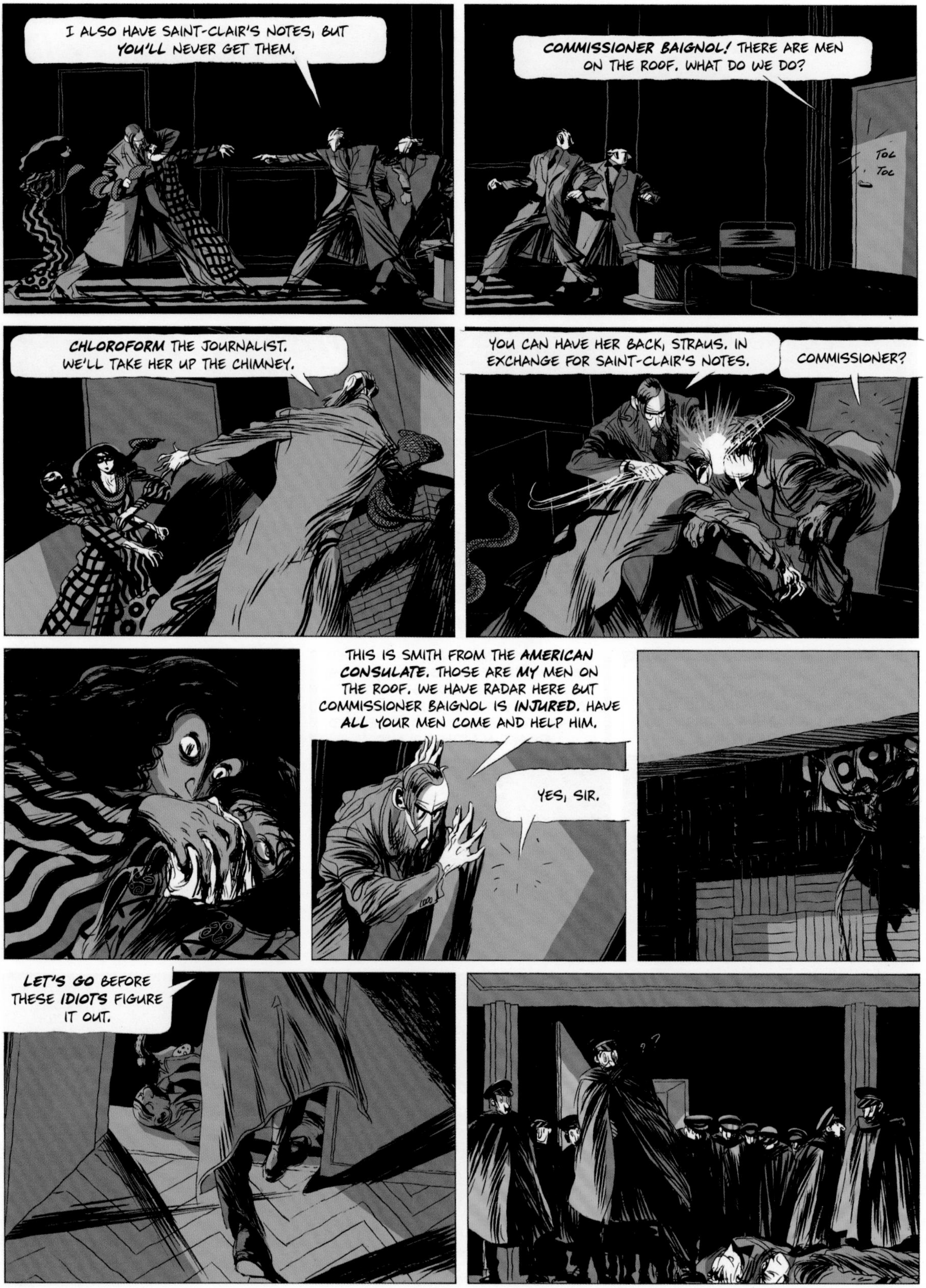
I ALSO HAVE SAINT-CLAIR'S NOTES, BUT YOU'LL NEVER GET THEM.
COMMISSIONER BAIGNOL! THERE ARE MEN ON THE ROOF. WHAT DO WE DO?
TOC TOC
CHLOROFORM THE JOURNALIST. WE'LL TAKE HER UP THE CHIMNEY.
YOU CAN HAVE HER BACK, STRAUS. IN EXCHANGE FOR SAINT-CLAIR'S NOTES.
COMMISSIONER?
THIS IS SMITH FROM THE AMERICAN CONSULATE. THOSE ARE MY MEN ON THE ROOF. WE HAVE RADAR HERE BUT COMMISSIONER BAIGNOL IS INJURED. HAVE ALL YOUR MEN COME AND HELP HIM.
YES, SIR.
LET'S GO BEFORE THESE IDIOTS FIGURE IT OUT.
? ?

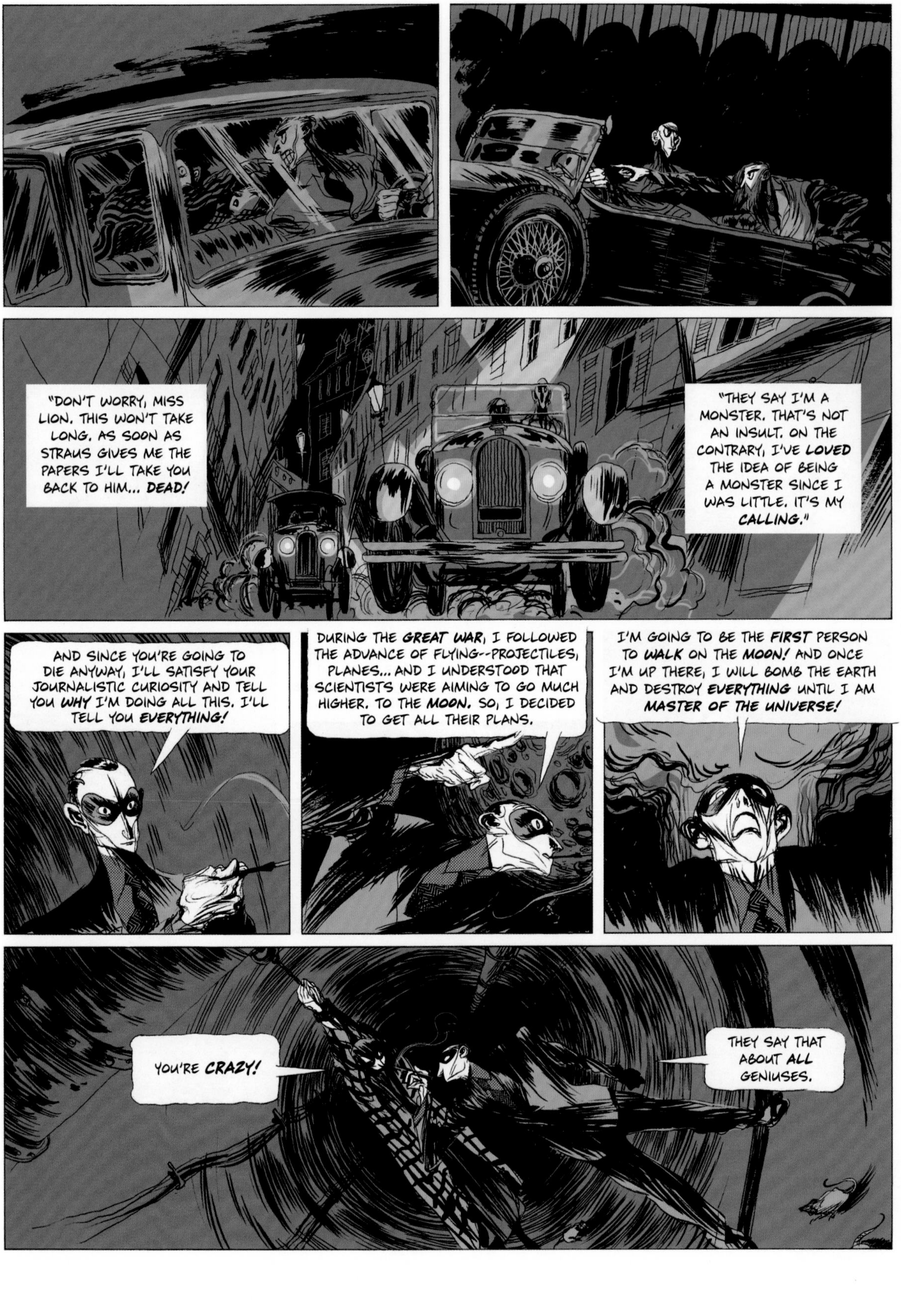
"DON'T WORRY, MISS LION. THIS WON'T TAKE LONG. AS SOON AS STRAUS GIVES ME THE PAPERS I'LL TAKE YOU BACK TO HIM... DEAD!
"THEY SAY I'M A MONSTER. THAT'S NOT AN INSULT. ON THE CONTRARY, I'VE LOVED THE IDEA OF BEING A MONSTER SINCE I WAS LITTLE. IT'S MY CALLING."
AND SINCE YOU'RE GOING TO DIE ANYWAY, I'LL SATISFY YOUR JOURNALISTIC CURIOSITY AND TELL YOU WHY I'M DOING ALL THIS. I'LL TELL YOU EVERYTHING!
DURING THE GREAT WAR, I FOLLOWED THE ADVANCE OF FLYING--PROJECTILES, PLANES... AND I UNDERSTOOD THAT SCIENTISTS WERE AIMING TO GO MUCH HIGHER. TO THE MOON. SO, I DECIDED TO GET ALL THEIR PLANS.
I'M GOING TO BE THE FIRST PERSON TO WALK ON THE MOON! AND ONCE I'M UP THERE, I WILL BOMB THE EARTH AND DESTROY EVERYTHING UNTIL I AM MASTER OF THE UNIVERSE!
YOU'RE CRAZY!
THEY SAY THAT ABOUT ALL GENIUSES.

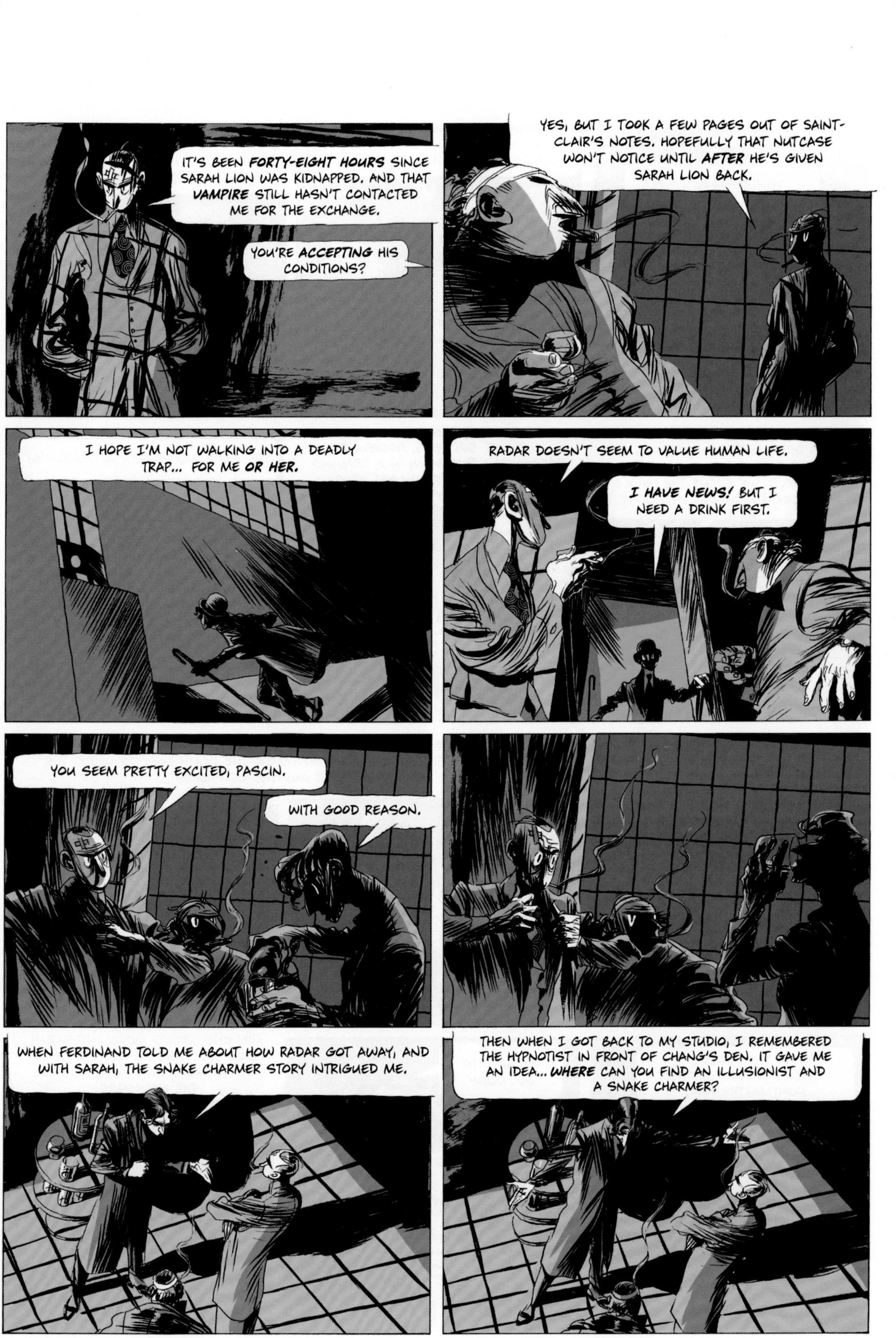
IT'S BEEN FORTY-EIGHT HOURS SINCE SARAH LION WAS KIDNAPPED. AND THAT VAMPIRE STILL HASN'T CONTACTED ME FOR THE EXCHANGE.
YOU'RE ACCEPTING HIS CONDITIONS?
YES, BUT I TOOK A FEW PAGES OUT OF SAINT-CLAIR'S NOTES. HOPEFULLY THAT NUTCASE WON'T NOTICE UNTIL AFTER HE'S GIVEN SARAH LION BACK.
I HOPE I'M NOT WALKING INTO A DEADLY TRAP... FOR ME OR HER.
RADAR DOESN'T SEEM TO VALUE HUMAN LIFE.
I HAVE NEWS! BUT I NEED A DRINK FIRST.
YOU SEEM PRETTY EXCITED, PASCIN.
WITH GOOD REASON.
WHEN FERDINAND TOLD ME ABOUT HOW RADAR GOT AWAY, AND WITH SARAH, THE SNAKE CHARMER STORY INTRIGUED ME.
THEN WHEN I GOT BACK TO MY STUDIO, I REMEMBERED THE HYPNOTIST IN FRONT OF CHANG'S DEN. IT GAVE ME AN IDEA... WHERE CAN YOU FIND AN ILLUSIONIST AND A SNAKE CHARMER?

VAUDEVILLE! OR IN A CIRCUS!

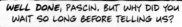

WELL DONE, PASCIN, BUT WHY DID YOU WAIT SO LONG BEFORE TELLING US?

I WANTED TO SEE MY SPANISH FRIEND, RAMON, FIRST. HE KNOWS EVERYTHING ABOUT CABARETS AND CIRCUSES.

HE HAS DOCUMENTATION WITH ALL THE NAMES OF PERFORMERS FROM AROUND THE WORLD. WE SPENT THE WHOLE NIGHT LOOKING FOR OUR HYPNOTIST...

...WITHOUT SUCCESS. HOWEVER, I RECOGNIZED THIS MAN, IN A DRAWING RAMON DID IN BERLIN LAST YEAR...

THE FAKE BARTENDER AT MAXIM'S!

Berlin 1919

THAT'S NOT ALL. HE DREW THIS AT THE CIRCUS.

RAMON TOLD ME ABOUT A FORMER SAILOR, LIKE ARTHUR, WHO'S IN THE PROGRAM. IT HAS THE LIST OF ACTS--THE LION TAMER, THE DEATH DEFYING BIKER, THE SNAKE CHARMER AND THE ILLUSIONIST.

MARCUS

CIRQUE MARCUS

HERCULE

JIM

KASSOURA

AND THE MARCUS CIRCUS IS PART OF THE MONTMARTRE FAIR.

WE HAVE TO GO, NOW!

NO! ONE WRONG MOVE AND SARAH LION WILL DIE. WE NEED TO WAIT UNTIL RADAR CONTACTS ME FOR THE EXCHANGE.

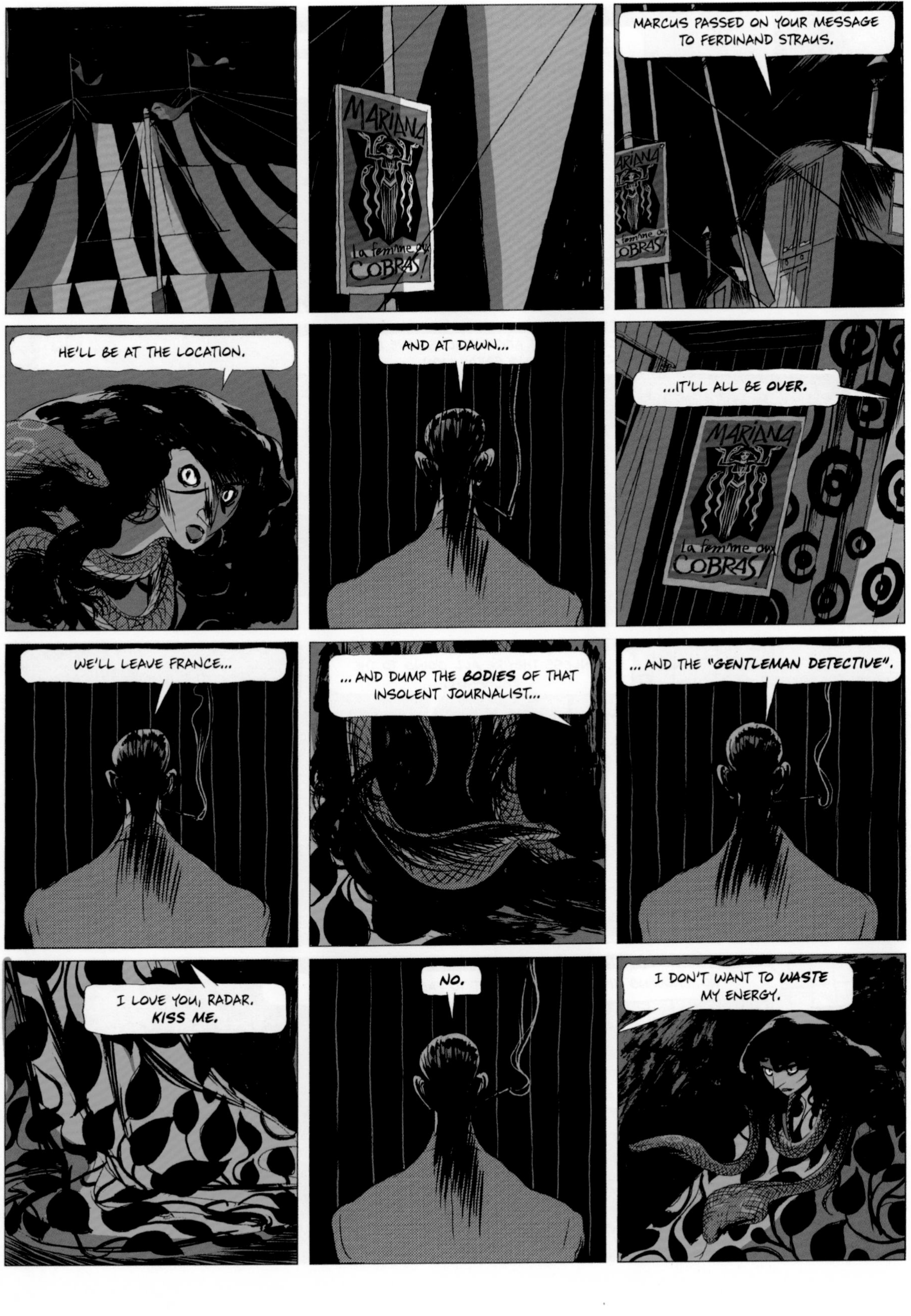
MARIANA
La femme aux COBRAS!
MARCUS PASSED ON YOUR MESSAGE TO FERDINAND STRAUS.
MARIANA
La femme aux COBRAS!
HE'LL BE AT THE LOCATION.
AND AT DAWN...
...IT'LL ALL BE OVER.
MARIANA
La femme aux COBRAS!
WE'LL LEAVE FRANCE...
... AND DUMP THE BODIES OF THAT INSOLENT JOURNALIST...
... AND THE "GENTLEMAN DETECTIVE".
I LOVE YOU, RADAR. KISS ME.
NO.
I DON'T WANT TO WASTE MY ENERGY.

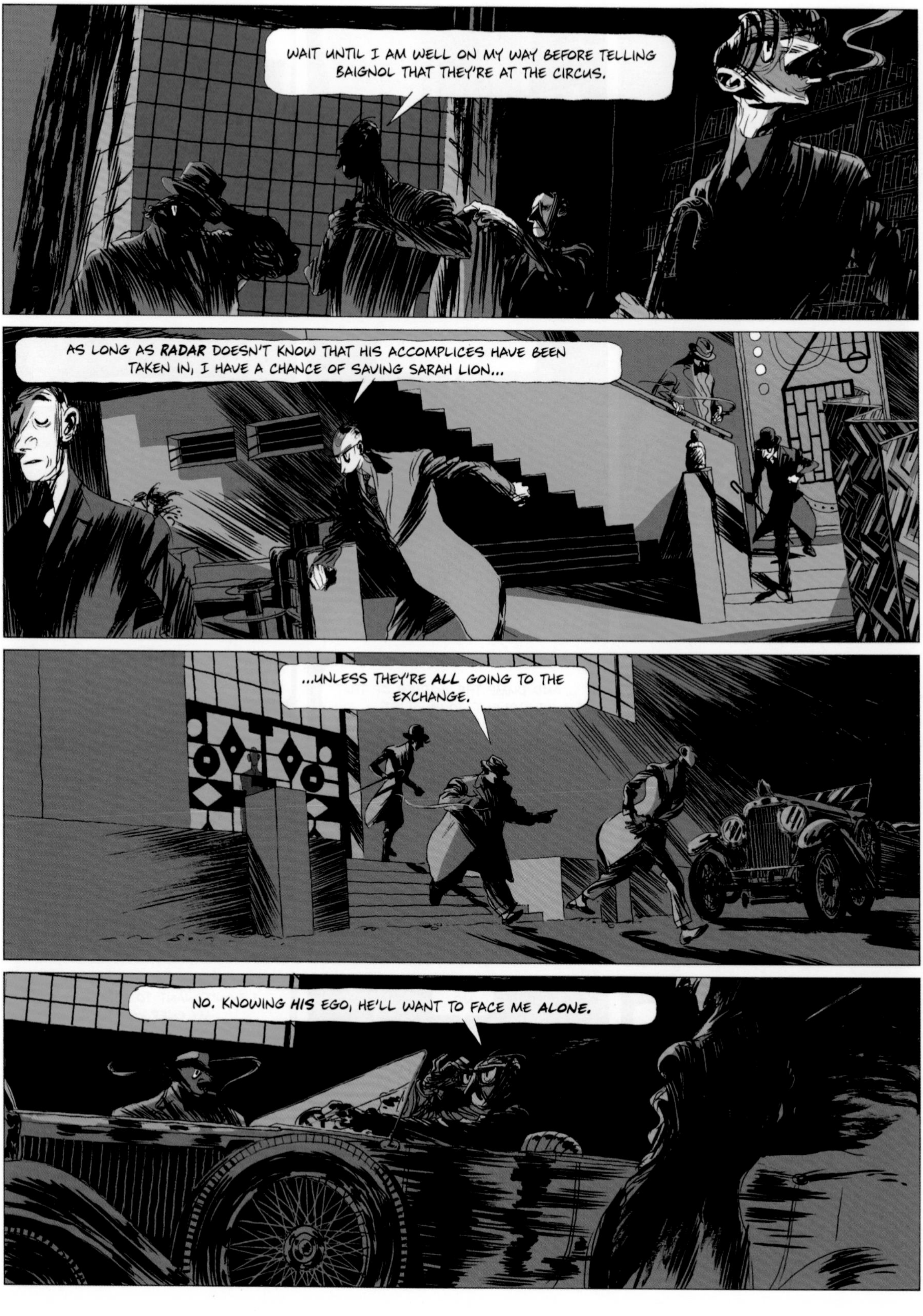
WAIT UNTIL I AM WELL ON MY WAY BEFORE TELLING BAIGNOL THAT THEY'RE AT THE CIRCUS.
AS LONG AS RADAR DOESN'T KNOW THAT HIS ACCOMPLICES HAVE BEEN TAKEN IN, I HAVE A CHANCE OF SAVING SARAH LION...
...UNLESS THEY'RE ALL GOING TO THE EXCHANGE.
NO. KNOWING HIS EGO, HE'LL WANT TO FACE ME ALONE.

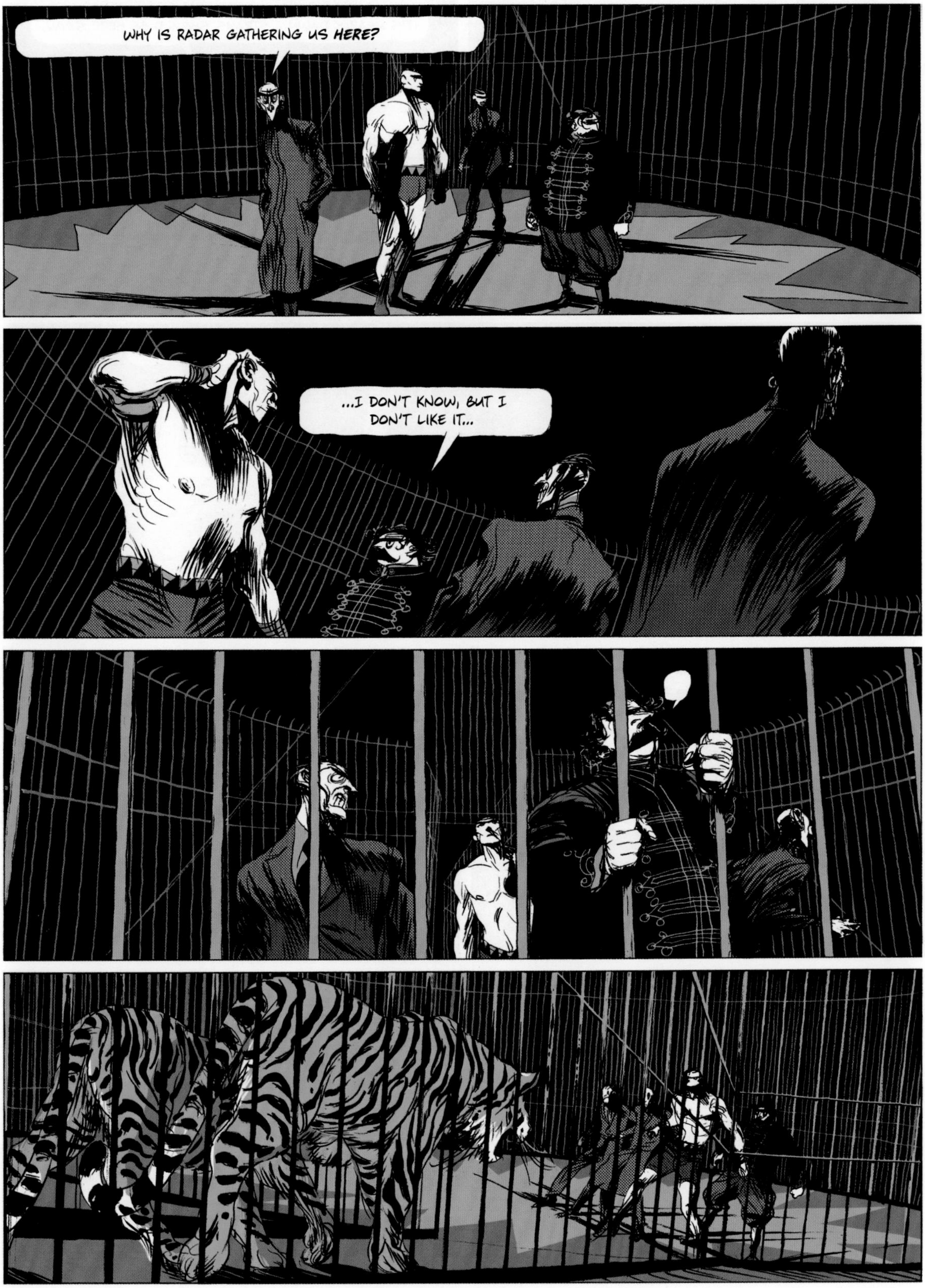
WHY IS RADAR GATHERING US *HERE?*
...I DON'T KNOW, BUT I DON'T LIKE IT...

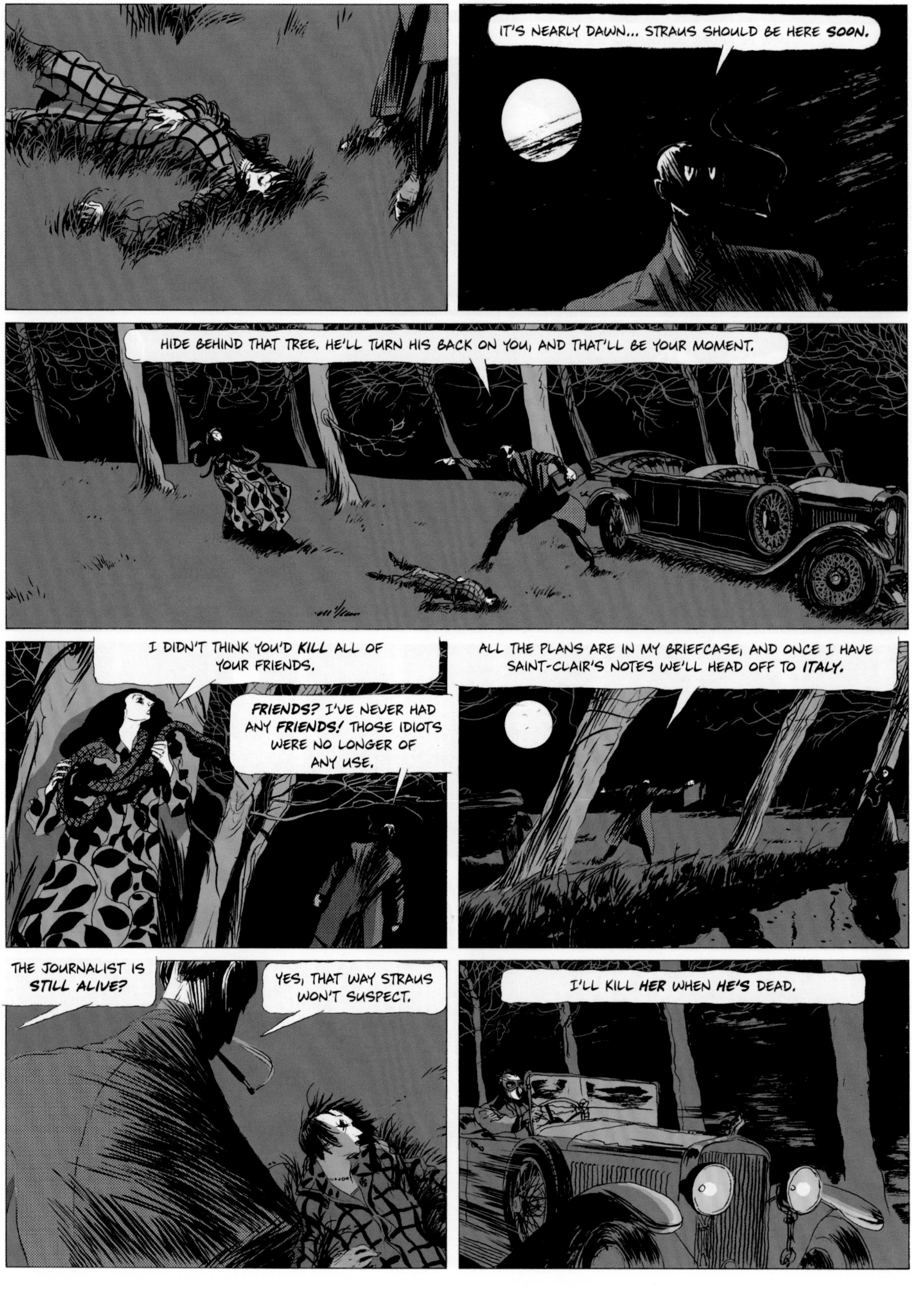
IT'S NEARLY DAWN... STRAUS SHOULD BE HERE SOON.
HIDE BEHIND THAT TREE. HE'LL TURN HIS BACK ON YOU, AND THAT'LL BE YOUR MOMENT.
I DIDN'T THINK YOU'D KILL ALL OF YOUR FRIENDS.
FRIENDS? I'VE NEVER HAD ANY FRIENDS! THOSE IDIOTS WERE NO LONGER OF ANY USE.
ALL THE PLANS ARE IN MY BRIEFCASE, AND ONCE I HAVE SAINT-CLAIR'S NOTES WE'LL HEAD OFF TO ITALY.
THE JOURNALIST IS STILL ALIVE?
YES, THAT WAY STRAUS WON'T SUSPECT.
I'LL KILL HER WHEN HE'S DEAD.

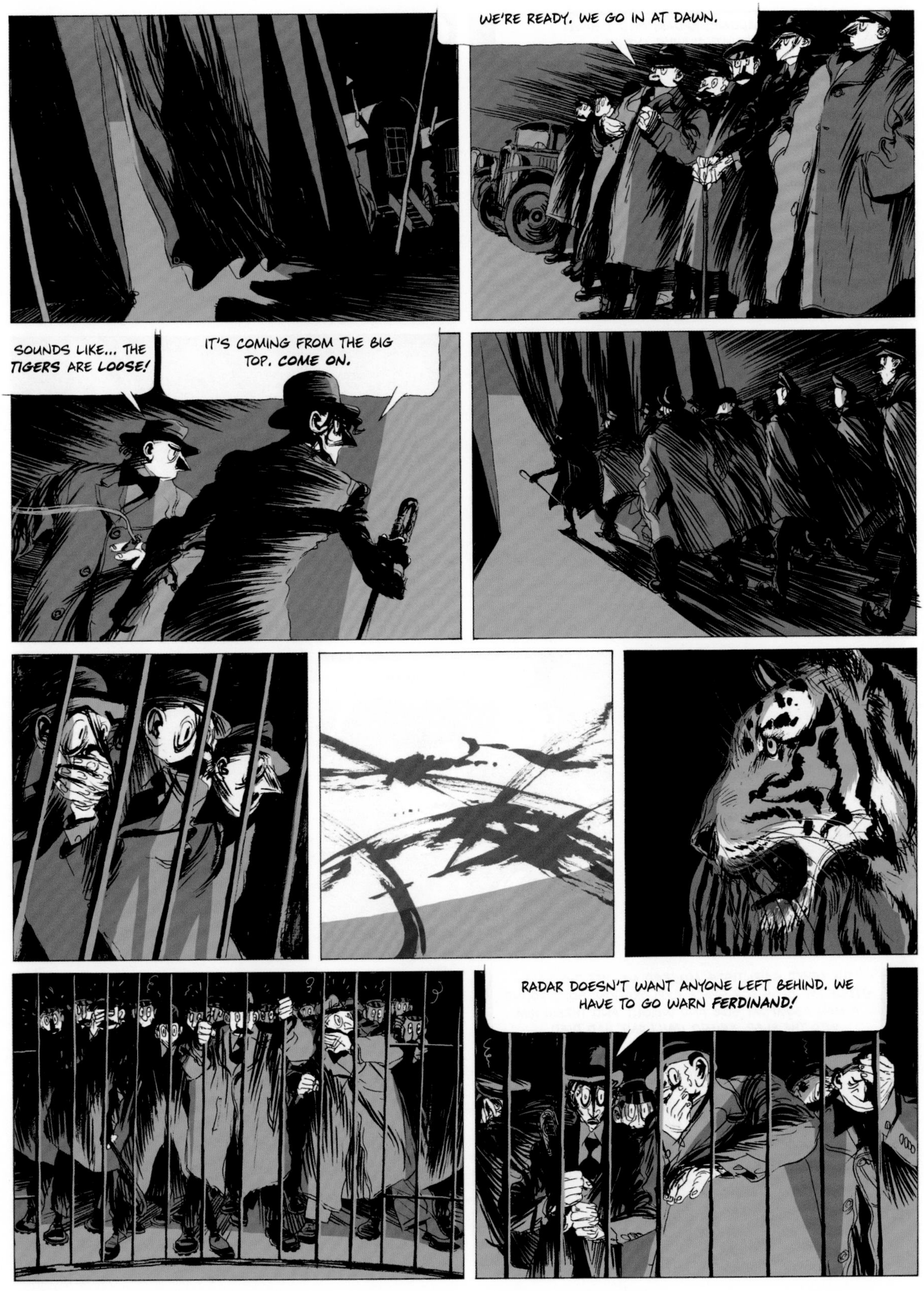
WE'RE READY. WE GO IN AT DAWN.
SOUNDS LIKE... THE TIGERS ARE LOOSE!
IT'S COMING FROM THE BIG TOP. COME ON.
RADAR DOESN'T WANT ANYONE LEFT BEHIND. WE HAVE TO GO WARN FERDINAND!

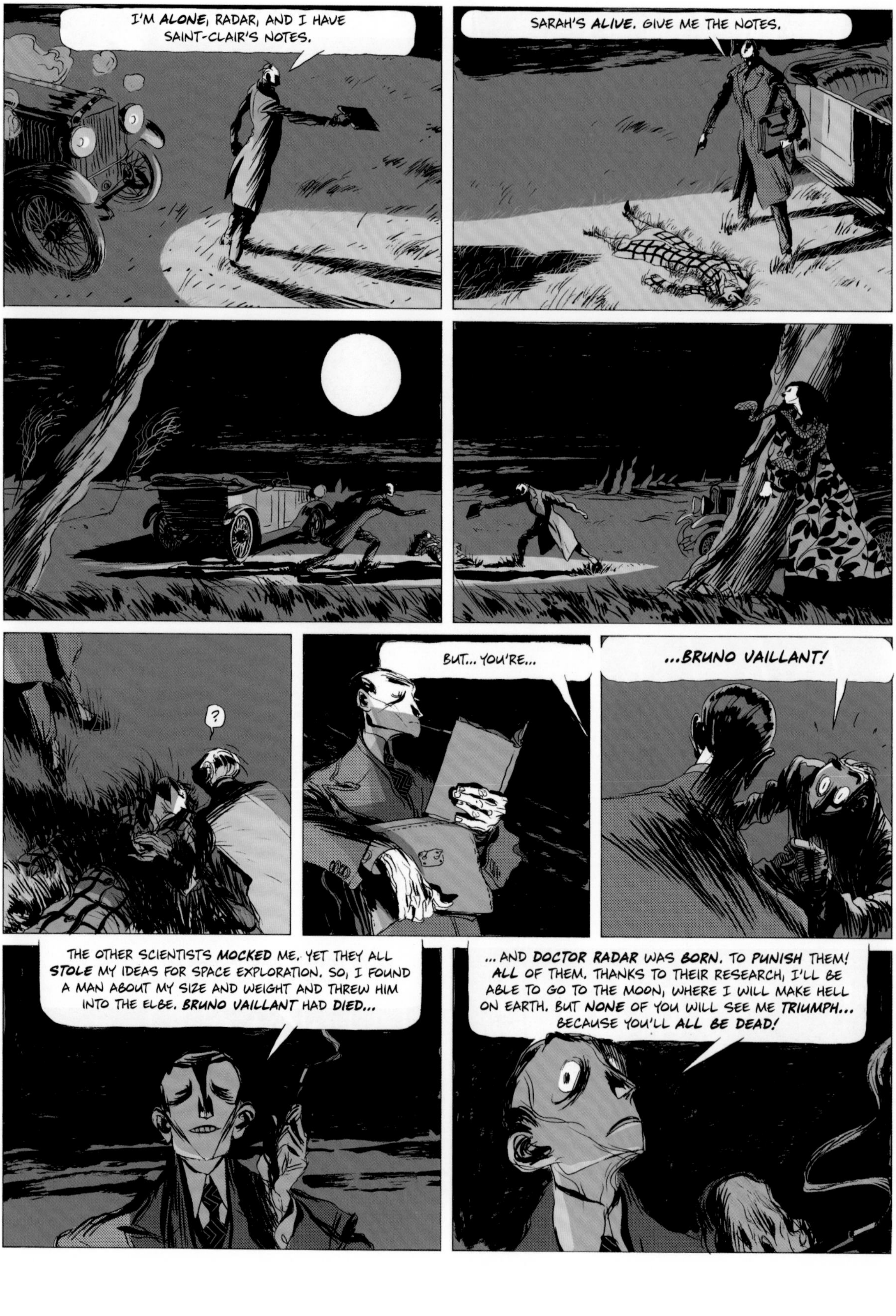
I'M ALONE, RADAR, AND I HAVE SAINT-CLAIR'S NOTES.
SARAH'S ALIVE. GIVE ME THE NOTES.
?
BUT... YOU'RE...
...BRUNO VAILLANT!
THE OTHER SCIENTISTS MOCKED ME. YET THEY ALL STOLE MY IDEAS FOR SPACE EXPLORATION. SO, I FOUND A MAN ABOUT MY SIZE AND WEIGHT AND THREW HIM INTO THE ELBE. BRUNO VAILLANT HAD DIED...
...AND DOCTOR RADAR WAS BORN. TO PUNISH THEM! ALL OF THEM. THANKS TO THEIR RESEARCH, I'LL BE ABLE TO GO TO THE MOON, WHERE I WILL MAKE HELL ON EARTH. BUT NONE OF YOU WILL SEE ME TRIUMPH... BECAUSE YOU'LL ALL BE DEAD!

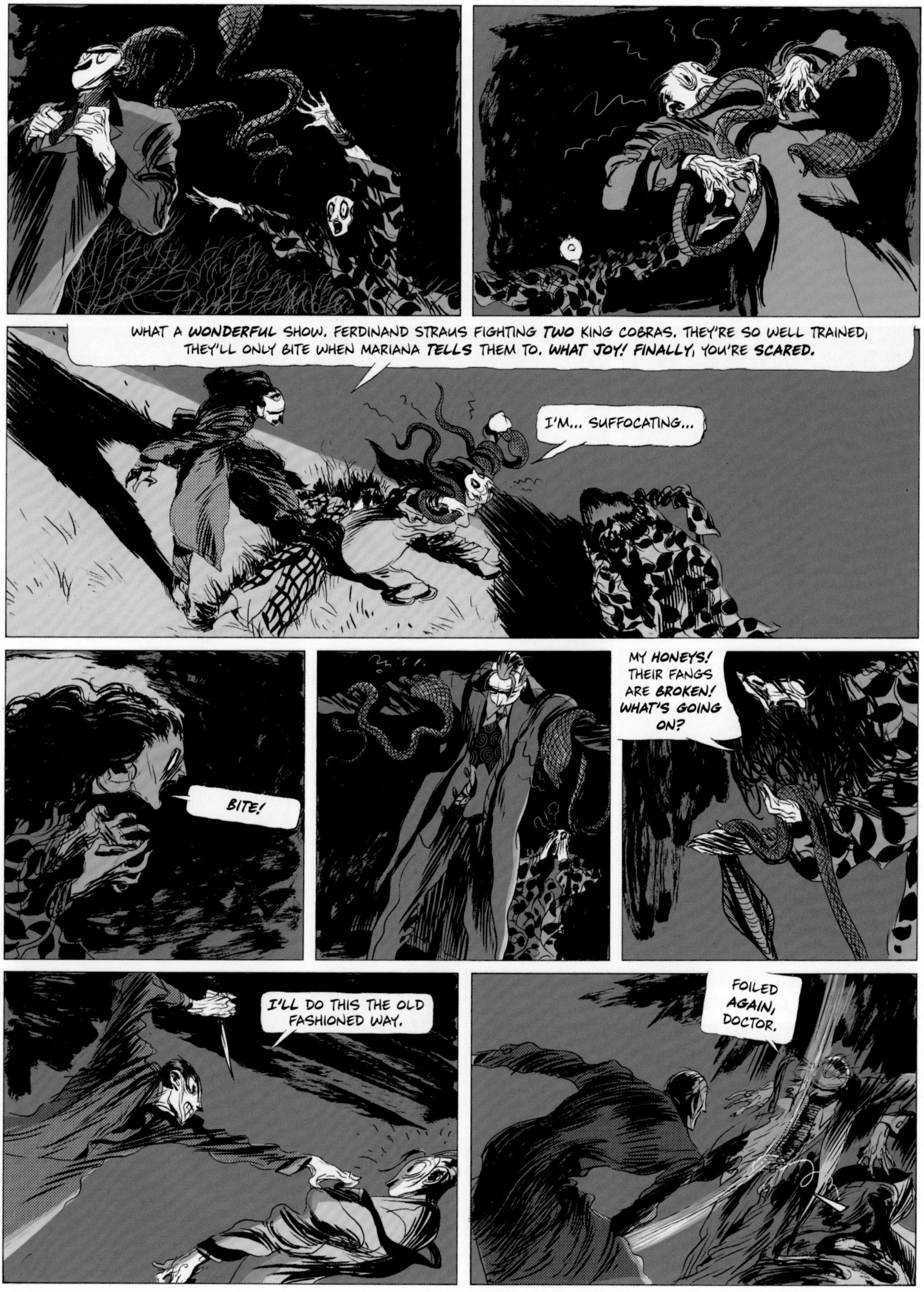
WHAT A WONDERFUL SHOW. FERDINAND STRAUS FIGHTING TWO KING COBRAS. THEY'RE SO WELL TRAINED, THEY'LL ONLY BITE WHEN MARIANA TELLS THEM TO. WHAT JOY! FINALLY, YOU'RE SCARED.
I'M... SUFFOCATING...
BITE!
MY HONEYS! THEIR FANGS ARE BROKEN! WHAT'S GOING ON?
I'LL DO THIS THE OLD FASHIONED WAY.
FOILED AGAIN, DOCTOR.

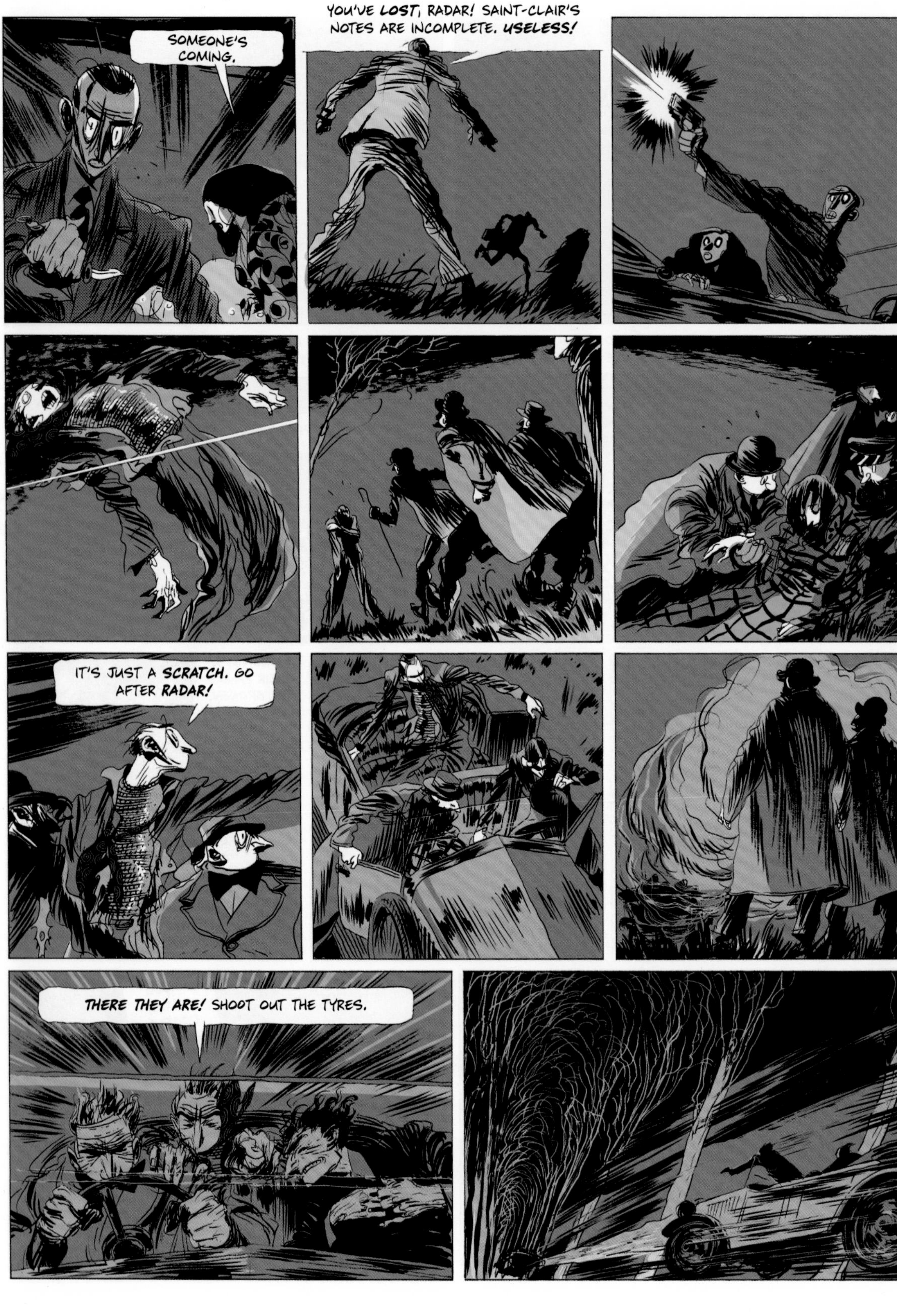
SOMEONE'S COMING.
YOU'VE **LOST**, RADAR! SAINT-CLAIR'S NOTES ARE INCOMPLETE. **USELESS!**
IT'S JUST A **SCRATCH**. GO AFTER **RADAR!**
THERE THEY ARE! SHOOT OUT THE TYRES.

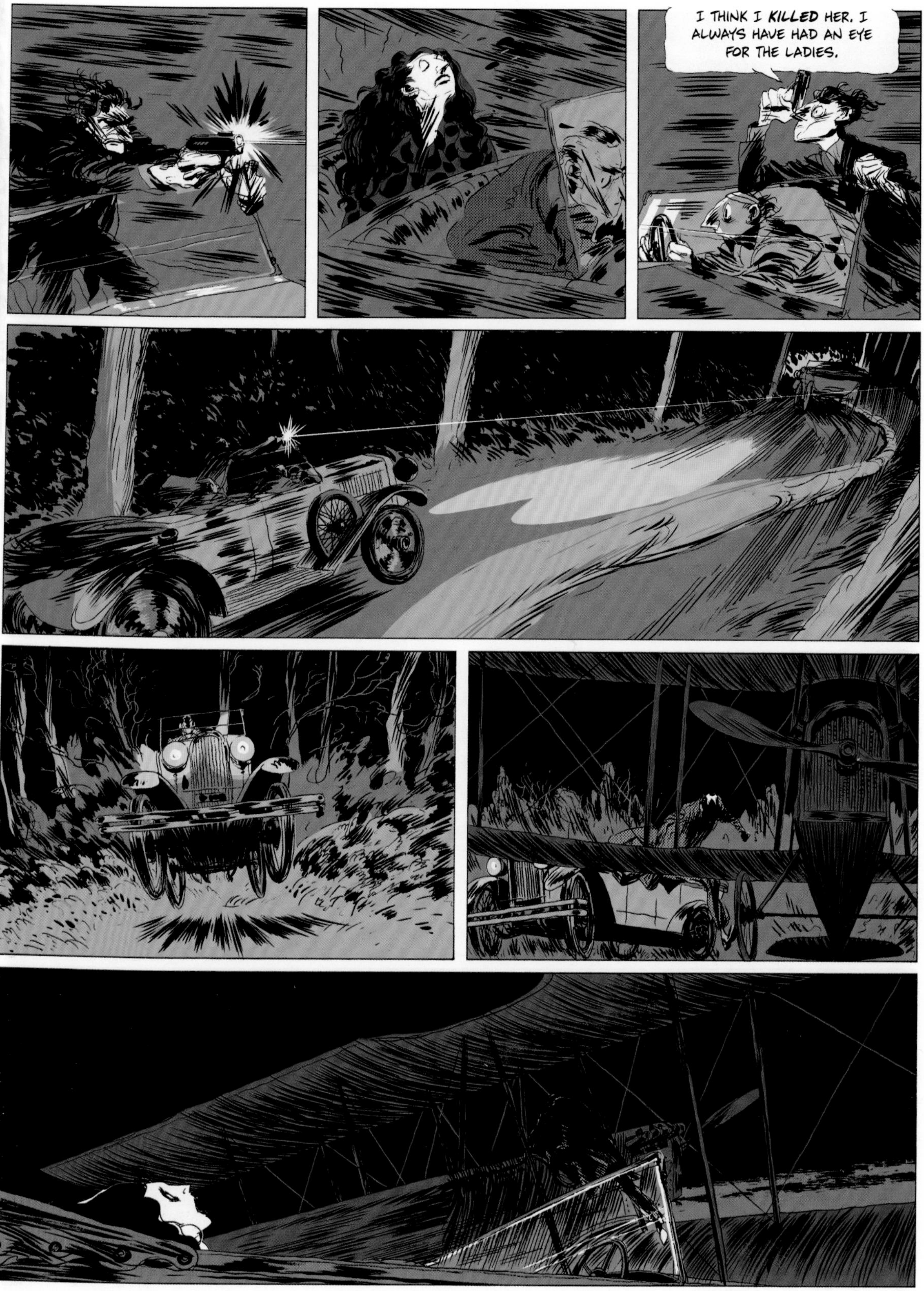
I THINK I **KILLED** HER. I ALWAYS HAVE HAD AN EYE FOR THE LADIES.

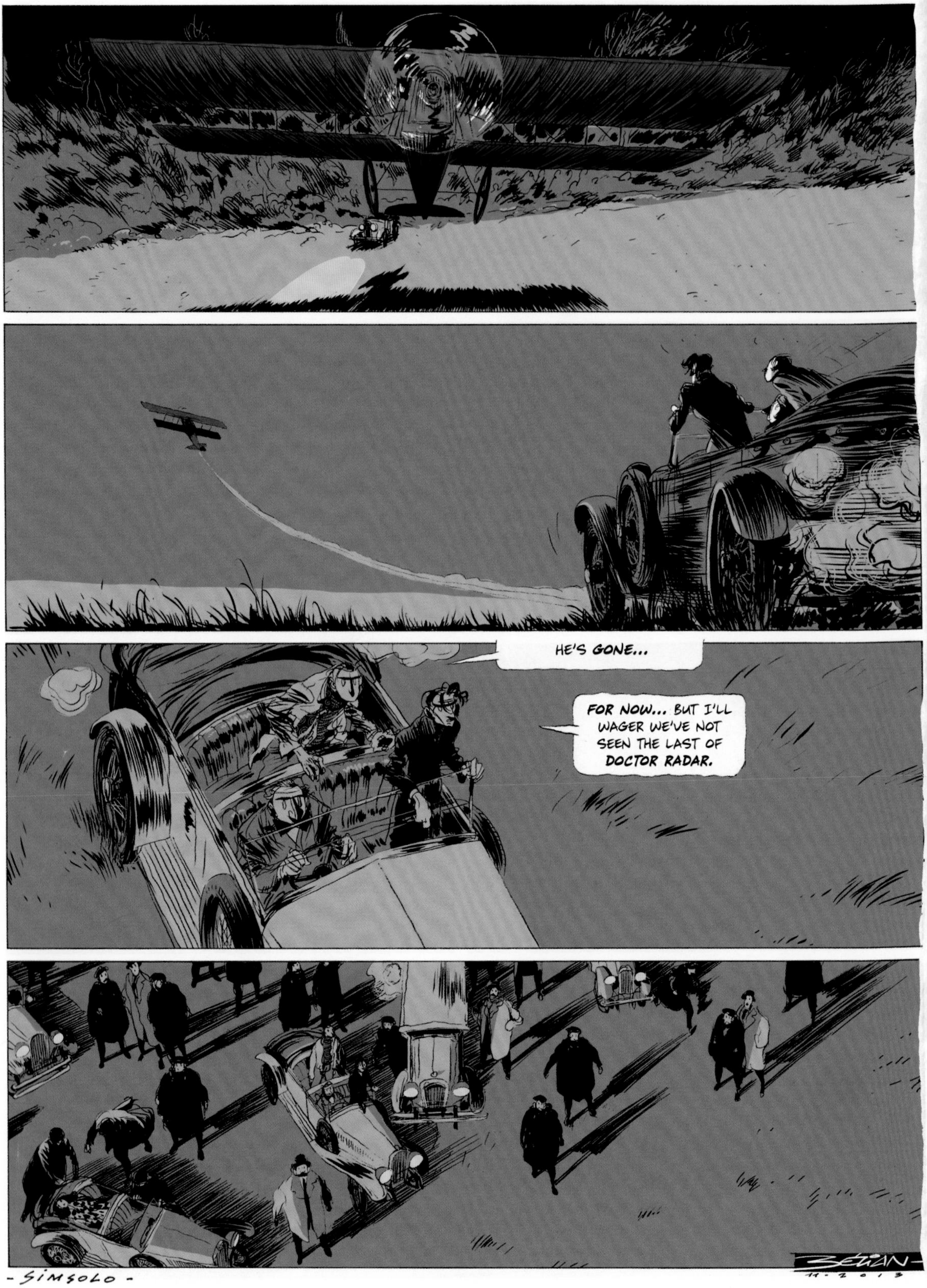
HE'S GONE...
FOR NOW... BUT I'LL WAGER WE'VE NOT SEEN THE LAST OF DOCTOR RADAR.
- SIMSOLO -
BEZIAN
11-2013

THE END.